THE FIRST 50 YEARS:
THE RETIRED SECONDARY
TEACHERS' ASSOCIATION

LOUIS O'FLAHERTY

The First 50 Years:
The Retired Secondary Teachers' Association

Published in Ireland by Drumcondra Publications, Dublin

©Louis O'Flaherty 2014

ISBN 978-0-9564110-1-3

Designed by Cliona O'Flaherty

Printed by Martone Press Ltd

The RSTA wishes to acknowledge the financial support given by Cornmarket Financial Services and the Dublin branch of the RSTA towards this publication.

GEORGE LODGE 1893 - 1968
FOUNDER OF THE
RETIRED SECONDARY
TEACHERS' ASSOCIATION

THIS BOOK IS DEDICATED TO THE MEMORY
OF GEORGE LODGE AND ALL THOSE RETIRED
SECONDARY SCHOOL TEACHERS WHO HAVE
CONTRIBUTED TO THE GROWTH OF THE RSTA.

Contents

Acknowledgements

I am indebted to the custodians, past and present, of the RSTA records, which are still retained by the association. A debt of gratitude is due to all past and current officers for the retention of minute books and other materials, which have proved most helpful in the compilation of this short history. Likewise I would like to thank the ASTI, and its General Secretary Pat King for access to its records and the manner in which I was assisted in its Head Office by Eileen O'Rourke. Ed Penrose, Joe Treacy and Moira Leydon gave me considerable assistance in accessing the earlier documents of the ASTI, which are retained in the library of the Labour History Society. I received assistance from Joe Lodge in my research into the career of his father and founder of the RSTA, George Lodge. Professor Michael Turner provided me with extensive documentation, which had been retained by his late father, Michael Turner. John O'Sullivan also provided me with a memo on Michael Turner. A special word of thanks is due to the honorary secretaries of the seventeen branches who helped me compile a short resume of the social activities in their respective branches.

This book could not have been written but for the two histories of the ASTI, which have been undertaken by Professor John Coolahan and John Cunningham and to both of whom a great debt is owed by all who are interested in the history of that organisation. Seán Fallon has been of immense help in transforming my manuscript copy into typescript and I am indebted to my daughter, Clíona who, not for the first time, has been responsible for the formatting and typesetting of my work. Indexing was undertaken by Dave O'Dwyer and continuous support throughout the project was provided by my long-suffering wife, Marie.

These are just some of the many people who have assisted me. Others who were helpful have not been mentioned and I trust that they will not be offended by the omission. If all were to be acknowledged this section would expand beyond the space allotted. To all who have assisted me I extend my sincere thanks.

Louis O'Flaherty
Dublin
February 2014.

INTRODUCTION

The working conditions of lay teachers in secondary schools in Ireland, at the beginning of the twentieth century were so bad that Dr. Starkie, chairman of the Intermediate Board of Education, speaking in 1911 said that "although many teach for a year, on the whole they are preparing for other work, no layman wilfully takes up teaching as a permanent occupation."

This was two years after the formation of the Association of Secondary Teachers, Ireland (ASTI) in 1909, which had expressly stated that its primary objectives were the securing of adequate salaries, a system of registration, security of tenure and a pension scheme. While the Intermediate Education (Ireland) Act, 1878 had instituted a system of payment to managers of secondary schools based on results and had also allowed for prizes to be awarded to the most successful students it gave no recognition either professionally or financially to teachers. This left lay secondary school teachers totally at the mercy of the managers of schools who could hire and fire at will. It was not surprising that in the period 1878 to 1909 numerous attempts had been made to organise lay secondary school teachers.[1] It would be wrong to say that the ASTI was pushing an open door in regard to the pressing of their legitimate aims and objectives but it is also fair to say that the deplorable conditions could not continue indefinitely. A Registration Council for secondary teachers was instituted in 1916 but the regulations did not come into effect until 1918. Incremental salary was not paid to secondary teachers until 1924. A pension scheme was initiated in

1929, twenty years after the introduction of a universal old age pension for those over seventy years of age. The percentage of the population living to seventy was very small and the percentage of secondary teachers who could hope to live to that age was probably even smaller. The new contributory pension scheme did offer the prospect of retirement at 65 subject to a minimum of ten years contributions.

While a pension scheme had been established, membership was not obligatory, and the benefits were often less than generous. The concept of pension as a form of deferred salary took root within the members of the ASTI. For many years there was a shortfall between the rate of pension paid to retired teachers and the salary paid to serving teachers. This remained a bone of contention with retired teachers and they sought to rectify it by lobbying their working colleagues to press their case.

From quite early on a pensions subcommittee had existed in the ASTI, usually a designated group drawn from the Central Executive Council and/or the Standing Committee. This group worked hard to improve the pensions of retired members. In 1952 a Pensioned Teachers' Association was formed. It was very loosely organised and there is little evidence of its activities and by the end of the decade it was moribund. In 1962, mainly through the efforts of George Lodge, the Retired Secondary Teachers' Association (RSTA) was established.

While the RSTA had its origins within the ASTI it has always retained a separate identity. Unlike its parent body it has welcomed retired members of religious orders into its ranks. It has not been structured as a branch of the ASTI although proposals for such re-organisation have been on the table in various forms since 1981. The RSTA lacks negotiating powers and must depend on the ASTI to ensure that the rates of pension and the continuation of parity with serving teachers is maintained. The ASTI has always been supportive of the RSTA and while the relationship between the two organisations has always been cordial there have been instances, particularly in the late nineteen nineties, when that relationship was somewhat fraught. Members of the RSTA have always supported any industrial action undertaken by their teaching colleagues and have been particularly active in organisations concerned with the welfare of retired workers. From its foundation members have participated in the Joint Consultative Council of Retired State Servants (JCCRSS) and later in the National Association of Retired Public Servant Employees (NARPSE) and more recently in the Alliance of Retired Public Servants (ARPS). The RSTA has been active in the Retired Workers Committee of the Irish Congress of Trade Unions (ICTU), the National Federation of Pensioners' Association (NFPA), and is affiliated to the Senior Citizens' Parliament. In addition it has maintained close links with the retired members of other teacher unions such as the Irish National Teachers' Organisation (INTO), the Teachers' Union of Ireland (TUI), the Irish Federation of University Teachers (IFUT) and the National Association of Schoolmasters / Union of Women Teachers (NASUWT) from Northern Ireland. These contacts have enabled the RSTA to keep abreast of all labour related developments that impinge on its members.

From its very beginning there has been a social dimension to the activities of the RSTA. Initially this would have started with coffee mornings organised by the mainly Dublin based group. This expanded to include an annual dinner. With the formation of new branches outside the Dublin area social activity increased to include local day trips, visits to theatres, lectures and foreign holidays to destinations such as New York. The RSTA is now a vibrant organisation with 1400 members in seventeen branches throughout the Republic of Ireland. As the RSTA celebrates its fiftieth birthday it is interesting to reflect that when its parent body, the ASTI celebrated its fiftieth birthday in 1959 its membership just topped one thousand members. It is to be hoped that the Retired Secondary Teachers' Association will continue to grow and represent the interests of retired secondary teachers just as the Association of Secondary Teachers, Ireland has protected the interests of serving secondary teachers for more than one hundred years.

CHAPTER 1:
BACKGROUND TO
THE EMERGENCE OF A
PENSION SCHEME FOR
SECONDARY TEACHERS

Irish secondary school teachers did not have the benefit of a pension scheme until 1929. Admittedly, they would have had entitlement to the modest state pension, which had been introduced in 1909 but they would not have been able to benefit from that until they were seventy years old.

The Molony Report of 1918 had recommended the extension of the English Superannuation Act of 1918 to Irish secondary teachers but their position was complicated in that they were not employed in the public sector but were in private employment. Their position was further complicated by the fact that a great number of secondary teachers were members of religious communities and the lay persons who were not had very fragile tenure in their jobs. The result was that while both national and technical school teachers had the benefit of a pension scheme this was denied to secondary teachers. The achievement of a satisfactory pension scheme had been one of the principal objectives at the founding of the ASTI in 1909. In the event the achievement of a registration scheme, security of tenure and seeking an incremental salary scale took precedence in the early years of the ASTI. These years were complicated by the historic events, which occurred at that time i.e. the 1913 lock out, the 1916 rebellion, the war of independence, the establishment of a new state and the subsequent civil war. The Central Executive Committee of the ASTI took the view that "as a matter of tactics and expediency it would be wisest to keep the pensions claim in the background for the moment so as to simplify the negotiations, to concentrate on the removal of one major grievance (salary)."[2]

Some satisfaction on the salary issue was achieved in 1925 and for a while the ASTI concentrated its efforts on the burning question of security of tenure. It had very little success in this matter due to the intransigence of their employers. It was only after further success on that front seemed unlikely that the CEC in February 1926 decided to "organise a vigorous and intensive campaign to support its claim for pension rights."[3]

It was probably not the best time to undertake a vigorous campaign on the pensions front as due to the chronic position of the state finances the Minister for Finance, Ernest Blythe had reduced the state pension by one shilling a week two years earlier. Nonetheless many retired secondary teachers were living in a state of penury if not abject poverty. Figures produced at that time showed that there were only 47 registered secondary teachers who could be deemed to be of pensionable age[4]. Armed with this information the ASTI and the Headmasters Association met with the Minister for Education, John Marcus O'Sullivan to seek to negotiate a pension scheme. While the initial response from the Government was not particularly favourable the ASTI received considerable support in the Dáil from the Labour deputy, Tom Johnston. After considerable lobbying the Teachers' Superannuation Bill was introduced in the Dáil on 12th July 1928. As noted by Coolahan this was merely an enabling Bill, which would permit the Minister for Education to prepare a superannuation scheme. This was cold comfort for members of the ASTI who were only too well aware that secondary school teachers in Northern Ireland had had the benefit of a pension scheme since 1922. This was doubly painful to them as some of these would have shared the same conditions of work before partition and no doubt some could also have been former members of the ASTI before the dissolution of the Belfast branch. The hopes of the ASTI members were not particularly raised when the Bill was introduced. The scheme would involve contributions from the teachers, the employers and the state and even the Minister for Education was less than enthusiastic about the Bill when he said "I do not pretend that the scheme is overgenerous and I am far from pretending that it will satisfy everybody. That is out of the question. I think that any scheme that we adopt will be such as the resources of the country will permit."[5]

The Bill fell short of the expectations of those who had lobbied for a proper pension scheme and speakers against the Bill included Éamonn deValera, who had been a steward at the inaugural meeting of the ASTI in the Mansion House in 1909 and J.G. O'Connell, General Secretary of the INTO.

Despite the fact that the heads of the Bill had indicated a three way contributory scheme the ASTI decided to look for a non-contributory scheme. The preferred scheme from the ASTI point of view would not only have been non-contributory but would be based on full pension after 35 years teaching based on the concept of one seventieth of salary for each year of service. The ASTI also sought that a pension would be received after ten years of teaching and that a gratuity would be payable to women teachers who retired on marriage. During negotiations with the Minister it became increasingly clear that he was unwilling to accede to the ASTI request and he repeatedly stated that secondary teachers were in a different category from civil servants and that the best that could be offered to them would be a voluntary contributory scheme. He was prepared to make some small concession to them in relation to the benefit that would accrue to teachers who had non-contributory years before the introduction of the proposed scheme. This was of crucial importance to older teachers and while the benefit was to be calculated at one hundredth of salary for each year of non-contributory service it was better than what had previously existed. After protracted negotiations the Secondary Teacher Superannuation Scheme was signed by the Minister for Education and became effective from 1st August 1929 and made retrospective to 1st January 1927. These two dates were to become particularly significant to secondary teachers in the following years. The 1st August became the recognised commencement date for the secondary school year and was always invoked as the determining factor for the allocation of posts based on seniority when they were introduced under the Ryan report in 1968. The fact that the scheme was initially made retrospective meant that in the future when teachers joined the scheme they were always entitled to buy back up to eighteen months worth of contributions.

The pension scheme that emerged was a compromise solution, which sought to recognise the complicated nature of the Irish secondary teacher's employment. The Minister had refused to treat secondary teachers in the same manner as civil servants and had consistently drawn attention to the fact that their managers were private employers. He insisted that the scheme be a voluntary contributory one between the State, the teachers and the schools. The teachers would contribute 4% of their standard salary and the schools would contribute 2.5% of basic salary. There was no indication of how much the State would contribute as there was no pension fund and pensions were to be met from current expenditure. The minimum period for which pension could be claimed was to be ten years but the normal retirement age was fixed at 65 years, subject to a maximum of 40 years service. There was no provision for a retirement gratuity or a marriage gratuity for a woman who retired on marriage. In those days it was normal for a woman to retire upon marriage and in fact the right for women secondary teachers to continue teaching after marriage was not conceded until 1973, after accession to the EEC. Pension was to be based on salary. There was to be no acknowledgement of inflationary tendencies on the cost of living index. This omission was to become very obvious in future years when pensioners on fixed incomes were to experience considerable hardship. There were considerable difficulties for older teachers when the pension entitlements fell short of their expectations. The ASTI continued to press for an improved scheme and when the Fianna Fáil Government came to power an amendment to the Superannuation Scheme was passed in July 1932, which enabled a number of teachers who had been excluded from the pension scheme to be included.

Despite the improved terms there was reluctance on the part of some teachers to join the scheme. As already noted more than 50% of the 1100 secondary teachers in the State were members of religious orders who were slow to join the pension scheme. They had the security of the communities in which they lived at a time when it was unusual for members of such communities to leave. Coolahan refers to the fact that of 450 lay teachers deemed eligible to join only 383 joined the scheme.[6] He suggests that most ASTI members who were eligible to join probably did and that the shortfall was accountable to the number of young teachers for whom a 4% cut in salary was daunting and retirement seemed a long way in the future.

The ASTI continued to press for improvements in the pension scheme particularly in relation to a clause which debarred teachers from benefit if they had been unemployed for two consecutive years. This was particularly invidious at a time of recession and when contracts of continuous employment were almost unknown. The Department of Education was reluctant to concede on this matter and cited their reluctance to the non-availability of an actuarial report on the true cost of the superannuation scheme. As Coolahan states "The ASTI got tired of waiting for the report of the actuarial investigation of the superannuation scheme."[7] In March 1939 the ASTI circularised all member of the Oireachtas expressing their concern about the absence of a retirement gratuity in the terms of the 1929 Act. The timing was particularly apposite as the scheme had been in existence for ten years and the negotiators in the ASTI had always regarded that Act as an interim measure towards the achievement of a much more satisfactory and comprehensive scheme. Yet again the ASTI was to be disappointed. In January 1940 the Taoiseach Éamon deValera stated that no improvements in the existing system could be made because of the financial situation existing at that time. A wages standstill order came into effect in May 1941 because of worsening economic circumstances associated with The Emergency. Some minor concessions were achieved in 1942 and in 1945 an ASTI deputation met with the Minister for Education to press for further improvements. They were seeking, not only a retirement gratuity, but also a death gratuity to the next of kin of a teacher who died before the date of normal retirement. The Minister appeared willing to concede on the death gratuity but not on the retirement gratuity. While slight increases were granted on the salary scales nothing was achieved on the pension front before the Fianna Fáil Government left office in early 1948.

Yet again the ASTI went into battle on behalf of retired teachers who had been fixed on pensions that had been determined on their salaries in the concluding years of their careers before retirement. Many retired secondary teachers were in straitened circumstances. Some were on pensions of less than £2.00 per week, which, even in 1946 was a very small some of money. At that time the maximum on the salary scale for a married man was just under £12.00 per week while that for women and single men was £10.00 per week. Admittedly there were complications, as so many retired teachers did not have entitlement to full pensions because they were in service before the pension scheme was introduced, had broken service or had not made sufficient contributions. This time the coalition government under John A Costello, having learned from the INTO strike of 1946, seemed more willing to listen to the demands from teachers. It granted ex-gratia increases of 50% to those on pensions of less than £2.00 per week, 40% to those on pensions between £2.00 and £3.00 per week and 30% to those on over £3.00 per week.[8]

In 1950 the ASTI re-opened negotiations with the Department of Education for improved salary and pension arrangements. Yet again the negotiators argued for the introduction of the maximum 35/70[ths] rather than the 40/80[ths] which had already been conceded. The salary issue was resolved first and the claim for improved pension was referred to the recently established Conciliation Council. The result was the Secondary Teachers' Superannuation Scheme, 1951, which became operative from 1st August 1950. The new scheme allowed for retirement and death gratuities to be paid in addition to disablement gratuities to those who were forced through ill health to retire from teaching and marriage gratuities to women who retired upon marriage. These extra benefits were to be funded by an extra 1% subscription by teachers. No advance was made on securing the 35/70[ths] for full pension. Nonetheless the scheme had become much more attractive to teachers, even though participation remained voluntary and quite a few teachers did not join.

The 1951 Superannuation Amendment Scheme became the benchmark for all future negotiations on pensions and the Conciliation Council was used to get further improvements for both serving and retired teachers. The Secondary Teachers Superannuation Scheme had only been in existence for twenty two years and those teachers who had joined at the beginning were not yet entitled to a full pension. There were many anomalies in the scheme and considerable distress was being experienced by many retired teachers. In the following year, 1952, it was agreed that final years teaching salary should be the yardstick for assessing pension entitlement rather than the average of the last three years service which had hitherto been the practice. This meant that pensioners got the benefit of any salary increases that occurred towards the end of their career but it still did not recognise the declining value of money or the impact of inflation on living standards.

During all these negotiations there had been a Pensions Sub-Committee within the ASTI, its most prominent members were Cathal Ó'Gara, Tadhg McCurtain and Dónal Ó'Conalláin. In May 1952 this committee suggested that a Pensioners' Teachers Association should be formed to liaise with the ASTI. This association seems to have had a very limited life and while it did liaise with the ASTI on some negotiations with the Department of Education in the early part of the fifties by the late fifties it was moribund. In 1959 the Pensions Sub-Committee was re-activated and it was decided to appoint an actuary to assess the benefits of the superannuation scheme. The actuary appointed was a Fellow of the Institute of Actuaries and in his first report, dated 26th June 1961, he said that the scheme was very good value. The report was examined by the Pensions Sub-Committee and after figures and statistics had been provided by Cathal O'Gara of that committee the actuary revised his opinion to say "that the benefits provided were only just value for money paid."[9] The Pensions Sub-Committee meeting of 2nd January 1962 noted that the final report from the actuary said that the pension and retirement gratuity were adequate for the increased rate of contribution from 4% to 5% since 1950 but that the compensation was not apparent in the death duty payable under the amended scheme and that an improvement should be sought.

What has been written here is an outline of the evolution of the Secondary Teachers' Pension Scheme as it had evolved up to 1962. I am deeply indebted to the scholarly work undertaken by John Coolahan in "The ASTI and Post-Primary Education in Ireland 1909-1984" from which source much of the material in this chapter has been drawn. However, there is more to the story of pensions than the recording of the strict chronological events. There are the retired teachers with very limited means who struggled to survive as the cost of living increased and their pensions remained static. One such teacher was Alice Burnett.

Alice Burnett had commenced her teaching career in the Holy Faith Convent, Chichester in 1908 but had returned to Ireland in 1915 and taught in a variety of schools until she secured a post in the convent of the Sacred Heart, Leeson Street, Dublin in 1929. Here she remained teaching until her retirement in 1951. On 20th September 1951 Miss Burnett wrote to Dónal Ó'Connaláin of the Pensions Sub-Committee stating that she had a pension of approximately £150 per year payable quarterly that was totally inadequate for the twenty years service out of her total of forty years teaching. She instanced the fact that a retired woman medical officer would receive £500 per year after thirty years service, a bank official £200 after twenty years and she asked that the ASTI would take action on her behalf.

The Dublin Branch of the ASTI tabled a motion for the 1954 Annual Convention which read: "That pensions and gratuities be calculated on the actual salary at the time of retiring and that it be dated as to include those retiring in 1951." This was an attempt to counteract the practice where pension entitlement was calculated on the average salary of the last three years before retirement. Not surprisingly the motion was adopted by convention but the ASTI negotiators failed to have it implemented by the Department of Education. Another resolution was submitted to the 1956 Convention at the instigation of Miss Burnett: "That further efforts be made to implement the resolution passed by convention in 1954." Despite the best efforts of the ASTI little progress was made on the issue and Miss Burnett kept up a constant correspondence with the ASTI in which she mentioned her deteriorating health and the erosion of her savings. In a letter to the ASTI president, Mr. Comerford on 30th January 1958 she said that while her pension had been increased to £172-3-0 her retiring salary had been around £600 per annum but because of averaging this had been reduced to £471. Her pension for twenty-seven years had been calculated according to that figure. It was a problem faced by many retiring secondary teachers at that time as some of their service had been non-pensionable or they failed to join the pension scheme.

Miss Burnett had been living in a small hotel in Harcourt St., Dublin but the last letter to her from the ASTI General secretary was dated 13th October 1959 to the Hospice for the Dying, Harold's Cross. It informed her that her case had been raised with the Minister for Education in March and that nothing further could be done in improving her pension entitlement.

CHAPTER 2:
THE ESTABLISHMENT OF THE RSTA AND THE CAMPAIGN TO OBTAIN PENSION PARITY WITH SERVING TEACHERS

At a meeting of the Standing Committee held in the ASTI Head Office, 36 St. Stephen's Green, on 24th March 1962 the General Secretary, Ms. Máire McDonagh reported that invitations had been sent to fifty pensioned secondary teachers inviting them to attend a meeting on 26th March for the purpose of establishing a Retired Teachers Association.

Branch secretaries were urged to forward the names of retired teachers in their areas to Head Office.

At the next meeting of the Standing Committee on 6th April a letter was read from the newly established Association of Retired Secondary Teachers thanking the Standing Committee and the General Secretary for facilities granted to them and reporting that George Lodge had been elected President. Miss F. E. Quirke, the former General Secretary had been elected as Honorary Secretary and Miss A Falvey as Treasurer. Other committee members elected were Miss M. Cotter, Messrs. J.G. Boylan (President 1940-1942), B. Joyce and H. Sadlier and it was proposed to have a further meeting on Monday 16th April at the ASTI Head Office.

It was noted on the Standing Committee minutes of 16th March 1963 that a joint meeting had been arranged between members of the The Vocational Teachers' Association (VTA), The Irish National Teachers' Association (INTO) and the ASTI for 21st March to discuss pension entitlements. It was also agreed to reply to various queries from the Irish Conference of Professional and Service Associations (ICPSA) regarding the Secondary Teachers' Superannuation scheme.

At that time the Pensions Sub-Committee in the ASTI was chaired by Mr. Cathal O'Gara who liaised with the Association of Retired Secondary Teachers, which seems to have had a very small and largely Dublin based membership. It was left to Mr. O'Gara to inform the Standing Committee of matters in relation to pensions and superannuation. At a Standing Committee meeting of 11th May 1963 it was agreed that he should convene a meeting of the Pensions Sub-Committee as soon as possible to consider the Superannuation and Pensions Bill, 1962 with a view to communicating the ASTI's observations to ICPSA. It was also agreed that a memo prepared by Mr. O'Gara on the Pensions Allocation Scheme be circulated to all members through the Branch Honorary Secretaries.

It would appear that there was some confusion as to the correct terminology and status of the newly formed Association of Retired Secondary Teachers. In the Standing Committee minutes of 15th November 1963 it is referred to as the Pensioned Teachers' Association. This was the name given to an earlier group which had functioned for a short time in the early 50s but which had ceased to exist. It was agreed that their annual subscription should be a nominal five shillings per annum. At the meeting of the 30th November 1963 a letter was received from the RSTA (sic) formally applying for affiliation to the ASTI. It was agreed to inform them that the ASTI representatives in Conciliation would seek to have pensions increased when salary claims are submitted. It was also agreed to point out to the RSTA that the Minister had already turned down a request that teachers over sixty-five be permitted to teach and draw incremental salary. It was also agreed that all Branch Secretaries should forward the names of those who had retired or were about to retire to Miss Quirke, Honorary Secretary of the RSTA at 24 York Road, Rathgar.

A meeting between representatives of the INTO, VTA and ASTI on pensions was held on 13th February 1964 and a letter from the VTA was read at the Standing Committee meeting of 21st March. Cathal O'Gara and Miss Blake gave a verbal report to the meeting and a written report was received from Tadhg McCurtain. It was agreed that the question of forming a joint deputation to the Minister for Education on pensions be referred to the CEC for decision.

In 1964 the RSTA President, George Lodge submitted a report to the ASTI Annual Convention in which he stated that the RSTA had been affiliated to the ASTI and he urged all retired secondary teachers to join the organisation. He went on to say that even though it was a small body, its association with the powerful Joint Consultative Council of Retired State Servants (JCCRSS) was of great benefit. He went on to say that not only was it unwise not to join the RSTA but "your self-respect must suffer if you are prepared to stand aside and take what the work of your fellows gets for you. Your Association is affiliated to the ASTI, thus giving the negotiators of that body authority to act for you."[10]

The ASTI refused to supervise or correct state examinations in 1964 and one member of the RSTA wrote to the ASTI informing them that he had sent a formal refusal to the Minister stating that he was unwilling to act as an examiner. A letter was also received from the president of the RSTA pointing out that compensation should be paid to their members whether or not they were still employed.[11] At the next meeting of the Standing Committee on 12th Sept. 1964 it was agreed that compensation should be paid to seven retired teachers who had refused to superintend that year and to four retired teachers who had refused to mark examination papers in support of the ASTI. The amount to be paid was undecided but it was agreed that the compensation should be paid whether or not they were working due to the inadequacy of their pensions. At a later meeting on the 1st Oct. 1964 it was agreed that retired teachers who refused to superintend should be paid £20.00 and those who refused to examine should be paid £50.00. Subsequently letters of thanks were received from seven of the eleven teachers who had been compensated (S.C. 24/10/1964) and two further claims were made. It was decided by the Standing Committee to inform these retired teachers that they should join the RSTA because it was that association which had espoused their cause. The general lack of money in the 1960s is evidenced by the fact that the payment of compensation to a widow teacher had to be deferred because of lack of funds. On the other hand, the General Secretary reported that one of the retired lady teachers who had been compensated had sent a contribution of £5.00 to the ASTI Benevolent Fund (S.C. 28/11/1964).

George Lodge continued to liaise not only with the ASTI Standing Committee but also with the Joint Consultative Council of Retired State Servants, which in a submission to the Committee on Post-Retirement Pensions on 23rd October, 1964 stated:

> A pension is not a gift from the State; in one sense pensions were clearly deferred pay and were part of the nature of remuneration that was paid after and not during service. State pensioners, who have the right to get their deferred pay in terms of the real value of that pay have also the right to share in the uplift given to serving officials on the grounds of increased national prosperity.
>
> It has taken nineteen years of effort by the public service pensioners to bring their cause from the position of abrupt Ministerial refusal to the present climate of Ministerial and public opinion. The statistical life of a (civil service) pensioner is 9.7 years.
>
> That septuagenarians and even octogenarians should have been forced to engage in this combat over the years is lamentable and it is confidently hoped that the Committee will consider and make early recommendations on the existing State pensioner' case, thereby at least lessening their burdens.

In his next report to the ASTI Annual Convention[12] George Lodge said that the JCCRSS had protested to the Minister for Finance, who had established a committee to examine the principles involved in making post-retirement adjustments in public service pensions but had omitted to include any State pensioners on the committee. Nonetheless the JCCRSS had submitted a statement of some 13 typed foolscap pages outlining their position to the committee. He also referred to the fact that the RSTA had supported the ASTI in the examinations dispute the previous year and acknowledged the fact that the ASTI had paid compensation to the retired members who refused to supervise or mark the State examinations.

All through the 1960s the disparity between pension payable to retired teachers and those still in service continued. The RSTA most notably through its President, George Lodge continued to make the case for retired secondary teachers. He noted that the 1963 Budget brought retired teachers to the same pay level as those who had the benefit of the pay rise of February 1st 1960. The 1965 Budget added approximately a further 9% - the actual addition was 14.5% to the pension of November 1963. Lodge noted that the Report of the Committee on Post Retirement Adjustments in Public Service Pensions was challenged on August 23rd 1965 and that they had sought a direct meeting with the Minister for Finance to put their case.

Despite the obvious efforts of George Lodge and his small cohort of active members, many retired secondary teachers were disinterested in the fledgling organisation. He complained that very few turned up at the Annual General Meeting to give ideas and moral support to the committee. He also made the case for closer liaison with their former colleagues who were still teaching. In an article entitled "The Pensioners' Case," published in the February 1967 edition of "The Secondary Teacher," he gave a comprehensive analysis of the plight of retired secondary teachers. He warned serving teachers that they should be mindful that some day they would be pensioners and that the fight being fought by current pensioners would then be theirs and that when that day arrived they would be powerless so they should act now to support retired members.[13]

At the fifth AGM of the RSTA, which was held on 22nd March 1967 George Lodge was somewhat more upbeat. While he regretted that he did not come before the meeting with definite promises of increased pension he felt that the atmosphere was not quite as depressing as it was the previous year.[14] He instanced the fact that the tenor of Ministers' speeches had indicated that their claims would receive more favourable consideration in the future and that it was difficult to see how a Minister for Finance could go on handing out the old plea that there was no money available when time after time he was able to find money when the demand was backed up with sufficient force. He went on to say:

> If our Christianity and our civilisation mean anything, every man should feel that justice will be done by him by society just as he expects justice within the manpower limits of his own family. If Christians are brothers in Christ the weak should be able to expect just treatment as surely as the weak ones expect it in the family circle. Jungle law must give way to the reign of justice coupled with mercy if Christianity is to survive."[15]

He lamented the fact that too many retired teachers were still outside the ranks of the RSTA and attributed this to their "I'm all right Jack" attitude as some of those who had recently retired had pensions of between £635.00 and £855.00 as against those who were longer retired whose pensions ranged from £400.00 to £540.00 per annum. He reminded these people that the value of money was still falling and that soon the value of their pensions would also decrease unless full parity was achieved. He said that the present officers and committee had been shouldering the burden since the association was founded and that in his opinion it was time for a change and that the current officers were willing and anxious to stand down in favour of new blood. The only reason that they kept going was to ensure that the association did not die and he wondered aloud if they were the only ones who wanted the RSTA to live.

The tone of the speech was remarkable, reflecting elements of deep religious conviction, social solidarity, commitment and regret. At that time George Lodge was seventy-four years old, having graduated from the Royal College of Science in 1916. He had taught physics and chemistry in St. Columba's College, Rathfarnham from 1921 to 1959. During his teaching career he had published school texts in Physics and Chemistry and had been one of the founders of the Irish Science Teachers' Association. From 1960 he had lectured students studying for the Higher Diploma in Education in UCD. As he concluded his speech he thanked all those teachers who had contributed to the RSTA funds and reflected that if they were more strongly supported they could make the AGM a more social occasion. It would be nice if they could afford to have a little standing buffet for this one night and meet one another on a more social footing, which, with support from all retired teachers should not be an impossible ideal.

The sense of frustration that George Lodge felt was even more apparent in his report to the Annual Convention some weeks later, when he instanced the fact that in August 1966 there were 430 retired secondary teachers drawing pensions, 214 religious and 216 lay, and out of the 216 only 65 had joined the RSTA. He instanced the fact that had he retired in 1966 instead of July 1959 that he would have over £300 more per annum in his pension. He said that it reflected very badly on retired teachers living in Dublin and its neighbourhood when only two or three other than the committee attended the Annual General Meetings in the last two or three years. His plea to convention was "We ask you to keep pressing that justice be done to us. They cannot as Christian men go on refusing when they are convinced that the injustice is becoming obvious to all and that you who are working are no longer prepared to condone it."[16]

Despite Lodge's plea for new blood at the 1967 AGM there were no new volunteers. The frustration is again noticeable in his report to the ASTI Convention in 1968. As yet there had been no major attempt to establish the RSTA outside the Dublin region. Even so if every retired secondary teacher within easy reach of Dublin turned up at the AGM they would not be faced with a meeting at which the committee was present with about five or six others, and having to elect the same committee year after year. He was particularly regretful that the RSTA had no representative at a recent important meeting of the Joint Consultation Council for Retired State Servants because of a combination of his being in hospital, another member being ill and the consequent failure to nominate a third delegate to the meeting. The sense of hurt was evident when he wrote that many retired secondary teachers were holding jobs in vocational schools but if they were ill they would have to absent themselves. They owe the rest of the retired teachers that service and it was their plain duty to attend and give that service. If they were not prepared to do that then they should write to the JCCRSS and resign their membership, saying that they were quite prepared to sit back and draw whatever benefits accrued from their hard and unselfish work. He concluded by recommending that they again read his article "The Pensioners' Case" in the February 1967 issue of "The Secondary Teacher."

This was the last report submitted by George Lodge. His health had been failing and he died in September 1968. In the RSTA 1969 report to the ASTI Annual Convention the new President of the RSTA, Mr. T. J. Boylan noted his passing and that of Eva Quirke, former General Secretary of the ASTI and then secretary of the RSTA. While expressing the sympathy of the RSTA members he wrote:

> Each of them worked unceasingly for the advancement of our cause, and their passing was a grievous blow to their colleagues. Even when George was sinking fast he constantly thought of the RSTA. In the last conversation I had with him he expressed the hope that the association should flourish and that our work should be crowned with success. Let us all join together to ensure that the last wish of our founder and President be fulfilled.

While the RSTA continued to press for full pension parity with serving teachers the bonds with the ASTI remained particularly strong. This was mainly through the continued assistance of the Standing Committee and the efforts of Cathal O'Gara,

Dónal Ó Conalláin, George Lyons and Tadhg McCurtain. Retired teachers were appreciative of the work being undertaken on their behalf by the ASTI. One such instance was a letter received by the Standing Committee in May, 1968 from a teacher who had recently retired due to ill health, in which he expressed his thanks to the ASTI for the services he had received and enclosed a cheque in appreciation.[17] After some discussion, at which the Standing Committee expressed its warm appreciation of the generous tribute to it, it was agreed that the cheque should be accepted. As a token of that appreciation arrangements would be made to send him a copies of "The Secondary Teacher"and Bliainiris in the future. This was the first instance on the part of the ASTI to send copies of its publications to retired members. While it did not as yet apply to all retired teachers or even members of the RSTA it was the forerunner of a policy that was to be adopted at a later date.

The 1960s had witnessed considerable changes in the structure and management of Irish second-level schools. This had begun with Minister Hillery's education announcements in May 1965 in which he indicated his intention to establish Comprehensive Schools. Later, Minister O'Malley's announcement of free post-primary education and third level grants coupled with the proposal to introduce Community Schools had an unsettling effect on teachers. There was widespread discontent with the salaries being paid and consequently to the pensions of retired teachers who still had not achieved parity with their serving colleagues. In an attempt to resolve outstanding salary issues the Government established The Tribunal on Teachers' Salaries (Ryan Tribunal) in January 1968. The Tribunal, unlike later tribunals, acted quickly and issued its report in May 1968. While the ASTI had hoped for improved salary and conditions what they were offered amounted to a reduction in salary for new teachers. In the event, the ASTI went on strike on February 1st 1969 for the first time since 1920. The strike lasted for three weeks and was supported by the RSTA who, when the strike ended, sent a letter to the President of the ASTI congratulating "the association in bringing the dangerous and delicate salary negotiations to a successful conclusion" [18] and enclosing a cheque for £10.00 for the strike fund. The Standing Committee decided that in view of the poor financial position of the RSTA that the cheque would not be cashed. The RSTA yet again had made a contribution to the serving teachers as they had done in the examinations boycott of 1964.

During the early 1970s the small group that formed the RSTA continued to meet and liaise with their serving colleagues but the numbers in the association remained small. This was frequently referred to in the annual reports, which emphasised the continuing disappointment felt by retired teachers who did not receive pension parity with their serving colleagues. While small improvements in pensions were acknowledged the frustration was palpable when the RSTA President T.G. Boylan wrote

"Promises and undertakings give hope but we cannot and will not be satisfied until we get that full measure of justice which is our due.

The small measure of justice meted out to us by the Minister has been delayed in its implementation by the lagging and foot-dragging of officials and up to the time of writing, February 10th 1970 no payments had been made to retired secondary teachers."[19]

All the work of these early members of the RSTA was carried out on a voluntary basis, as it continues to be to this day. There was no scheme of early retirement and many of the activists were in their late sixties and early seventies. Money was scarce and participation with other similar interest groups imposed considerable demands on the small cohort of active members. Money was always a problem and while the annual subscription to the RSTA had remained at 50p costs had increased.

In November 1971 the RSTA wrote to the Standing Committee of the ASTI seeking a subvention due to the increased demands on their finances and their participation in the Retired State Pensioners' Association. The Standing Committee agreed to give them a grant of £30.00 which was duly acknowledged. This was the start of an annual subvention, which has increased over the years.[20]

Mr T. G. Boylan resigned as President of the RSTA in 1971 and was succeeded by Mr. Patrick Hardiman. Both of these men had been former presidents of the ASTI, T. J. Boylan in 1940 and 1941 and Patrick Hardiman in 1956. They had kept the ASTI afloat in its dark days and they continued to assist the RSTA after their retirement.

In his annual report to the ASTI Annual Convention in 1973 Hardiman stated that the RSTA in association with the JCCRSS had intensified its campaign for full pension parity over the previous year. He said that they had assumed from Mr. Colley's budget statement in 1972 that full parity would be granted on January 1st 1973 and paid on October 1st 1973 and that thereafter adjustments in pensions would operate automatically in conformity with adjustments in the salaries of serving teachers. This had not happened and it appeared that the parity issue was only applicable for three months from October 1st 1972 to January 1st 1973. It appeared that if rates of pay increased at the end of June of any year, pensioners would have to wait until October 1st in the following year for payment. This was something less than parity at a time of rapidly increasing inflation and became known as "the lag." The JCCRSS decided to pursue the claim "that all adjustments in pay for serving members be followed automatically by corresponding adjustments in the pensions of retired officers of corresponding status and that they will operate from the same date."[21]

The campaign for parity was continued by the ASTI, which in addition sought the reintroduction of a scheme whereby teachers could buy back pensionable service as a quid pro quo for the superannuation scheme becoming compulsory.[22] The RSTA was unhappy with the time lag and sought an interview with the Minister for Education Mr. Richard Burke, who had been a prominent member of the ASTI and who, it was hoped, would be sympathetic to their cause. A letter was sent to Mr. Burke "requesting a meeting with him to discuss the discrepancy or lag between payment increases to serving teachers and the retired members." [23] The reply from the Minister was deemed to be "completely irrelevant and evasive"[24] and it was the opinion of the RSTA that there was no point in sending a deputation to meet the Minister. Despite the decision not to send a delegation to the Minister for Education, President Hardiman was able to report to the ASTI Convention in 1974 that, as of October 1st 1973, retired teachers on maximum pension received an increase of 14% and for those with lower pensionable service the percentage increase was slightly less.[25] He regretted that there had been no improvement on the undertaking that pension increases would operate from the same date as that applicable to serving teachers. He said that retired public servants still had to wait a minimum of three months and a maximum of sixteen months for their increases. This was in contrast with the views of Mr. Ryan, Minister for Finance when he was in opposition and he regretted that they were no nearer parity than they were under their predecessors in office. Minister Ryan had written to the JCCRSS on

November 30th saying, "You may be assured that the Government will take the necessary steps to honour the pledges already given on its behalf."

Despite the lobbying by the RSTA and the ASTI very little progress was made in eliminating the lag between the payment of pension increases and salary increases to serving teachers. Patrick Hardiman, President of the RSTA was able to report to the Annual Convention of the ASTI that the financial position of retired teachers had improved dramatically as a result of the adoption of parity with those currently retiring. He reflected that while it would be pleasing to record that the basic demand was conceded graciously and easily by the Government, in fact it took a long campaign of constant pressure to obtain it, that the details of the scheme left much to be desired and that there was still a need for organisation and unity to fight for financial security.[26] He referred to the massive increase in the cost of living, which he said was running at 25% per annum. He instanced the fact that while pension increases were announced on July 1st, they were not paid until October 1st. However the teachers' salaries upon which pensions were calculated could have been increased quite a time before July 1st resulting in a delay of up to 15 months before the increase was awarded to pensioners.[27]

While all this was going on the RSTA remained a very small organisation of very dedicated members. At a meeting in March 1975[28] the treasurer Mr. Henry reported that while the balance in the bank of approximately £125 was quite satisfactory there had been a decline in the number of subscribing members of 60% from 57 to 22 in recent years. It was decided to try and organise the association in the provinces where contact with Dublin was almost non-existent. Messrs Hardiman and Coppinger offered their services in the re-organisation plan. It was felt that they had not yet sufficient publicity for the lag in payment of pension increases and it was suggested by Miss McAllister that they should be more aggressive in dealing with the Minister and that recourse should be taken to the media and to the radio in particular. It was decided that that was not feasible and wouldn't serve the purposes of the RSTA. Only six members were present at the next meeting of the RSTA even though quite a few had been notified.[29] No lady member was present and it was announced that Mr. Henry, the former treasurer had gone to live in England and that he had been replaced by Eric Simmons. At the same time the annual subscription had been raised to £1.00 which was supplemented by a subvention from the ASTI. During the late 1970s the meetings of the RSTA became increasingly infrequent. The same small group of committed members continued to meet and tried to exert as much pressure as possible so that there would be a complete synchronisation of pension increases with those of serving teachers.

One development which might have helped in the achievement of that goal was the proposal from retired members of the INTO to form an Association of Retired Teachers which would include retired members of the INTO, TUI and ASTI. It was a reasonable proposal seeing that a common basic salary had been in operation for nearly ten years and all three teacher unions were members of the Irish Congress of Trade Unions.[30] O Conalláin was of the opinion that copies of the proposals for the draft constitution of the proposed new organisation should be obtained and should be discussed at a meeting in September 1978.[31] It was also stated that if the RSTA were to become part of a larger organisation that it might require an increase in the annual subscription.

In the event that meeting did not take place and while Hardiman continued to report to the ASTI Annual Convention no further meetings of the RSTA were convened until September 1981.

CHAPTER 3:
REVIVAL AND RESURGENCE
1981-1993

In September 1981 a group of 22 retired secondary teachers and former members of the ASTI, including members of the RSTA, conscious of the fact that the RSTA had not held a meeting for over three years and believing that organisation to be moribund, convened a meeting of interested parties to be held in the ASTI head office on September 29th 1981 at 3.00.pm.

Thirteen retired teachers including Patrick Hardiman attended and there were apologies from a further thirteen. Six of those present were former presidents of the ASTI. At the outset of the meeting a very detailed discussion arose as to whether those present were empowered to proceed with the agenda. Mr. Coppinger protested that the meeting was irregularly convened in that the terms of the constitution providing for the calling of a General Meeting had been contravened. He argued that no valid decisions could, therefore, be arrived at. He proposed that the meeting adjourn and that a properly convened meeting be arranged at an early date. This proposal received no support from those present apart from the chairman, Mr. Hardiman. The general view was that a mere procedural issue should not be allowed "to thwart a genuine effort to re-establish an association which through ineptitude and inaction on the part of its chief officer had already become defunct."[32] It was pointed out that the same constitution that was being so glibly invoked to invalidate the meeting had been utterly ignored since Mr. Hardiman's accession to the office of President in that he had never convened an AGM or done anything at committee

entitle them to the services of the ASTI on their behalf. He said that a committee had been established to see how best the resolution could be implemented and that the committee was to report to the Christmas CEC meeting of the ASTI. The retained minutes of the RSTA are incomplete on this topic and seem to finish rather abruptly. There is also some confusion as to the sequence of the events recorded as the lunch and AGM had preceded the annual ASTI Convention by some weeks. There can be little doubt that Ó'Conalláin reported on the events of the ASTI Convention but it was probably at a subsequent meeting and unfortunately Mr. Hannigan, the Honorary Secretary died during that summer, which could account for the confusion and apparent contradiction in the recorded minutes.

While the adoption of Motion 293 by Annual Convention was welcomed there was another development at the Wexford Convention, which caused considerable annoyance to the RSTA. Since 1964 it had been the custom to print a report of the Retired Secondary Teachers' Association in Section VIII of the ASTI Convention Handbook. This had been done by all presidents of the RSTA each year and was continued by Mr. Hardiman even in those years when no meetings had been called.

The 1982 report penned by Dónal Ó'Conalláin outlined the events which had occurred in the RSTA in the previous year but was particularly critical of the performance of Mr. Hardiman, the previous president, saying:

> "No communication had been issued for years on the progress or otherwise of negotiations for the redress of our major grievances and, in flagrant violation of the vaguely known Rules and Constitution of the RSTA, no Annual General Meeting had been called for several years."[36]

At that time reports to ASTI Conventions were usually formally proposed and adopted. Not so in this case. No sooner had the report been proposed by Mr. Michael Ward, Treasurer of ASTI and seconded by Mr. W. Ruane of West Mayo than it was opposed by Mr. Tony Weir, who said that "it cast an unhappy light on Mr. Hardiman and on the fact that the September meeting referred to in that report was an illegal one."[37]

Mr. M. Mullen, delegate from Dun Laoghaire also opposed the adoption of the report and he said it was "loaded with innuendo and contained a personal attack on a past president of this association."[38] The report was put to Convention and rejected. This was a setback to the rejuvenated RSTA as no opportunity to defend the report had been given at Convention and as a result no further printed RSTA reports to Convention were made until 2012, when a very brief note was included in the Annual Convention Handbook. From then on the activities of the RSTA were conveyed to ASTI members through the RSTA notes which appeared regularly in ASTIR.

Ó'Conalláin threw himself into the position of President with gusto. He established firm connections with the ASTI, arranged for the distribution of ASTIR to the members and contributed a column to every issue of that journal. He re-invigorated RSTA participation in the Joint Consultative Council of Retired State Servants and he was particularly interested in developing the social side of the RSTA. He moved easily between the retired teachers and those who were still at the chalk face. Despite all this there was very little increase in the overall numbers of the RSTA. There is hardly a set of minutes of a meeting that does not record the death of one of the members and new recruits did little more than keep the numbers fairly static. The strain of long years of teaching, modest pay and an unsatisfactory pension scheme continued to take its toll on the members.

That stress was somewhat relieved in 1984 when Mr. Alan Dukes, Minister for Finance, announced in his budget in March that in the future pension adjustments in the public service would be made to synchronise with corresponding salary adjustments. That had been the objective of the RSTA for many years but writing in ASTIR Ó'Conalláin sounded a note of warning: "We should really be jubilant that it has come so soon . . . However, our work as an association is not yet complete. Attention must now be directed at getting awards paid within a reasonable time."[39] This was a reference to the "lag" between the granting of an increase and the payment to retirees. He blamed the Pensions Section of the Department of Education for the delay and its excuse that it was caused by the volume of work. He went on to say: "With all the gadgetry now available in the name of technology for expediting calculations even of the most complex kind, the volume of work plea is totally unacceptable."[40]

At a committee meeting on April 21st 1983 it was decided to ask Timothy Holland of Cork and Sorcha O'Halloran of Galway to assist in the distribution of the ASTIR. At the time ASTIR was delivered in bulk to the RSTA which in turn distributed or posted it to the members. This was quite time consuming for the members and the new proposal would lessen the burden on the Dublin based members but would also be an attempt to involve more people from outside Dublin in the organisation. The attempt met with some success and it was decided to hold the 1984 AGM in Galway. The meeting was held in the Great Southern Hotel on March 28th and nearly thirty members attended, not only from Dublin and Galway but also from Donegal, Nenagh, Wicklow and Kerry. The RSTA had finally broken out from the confines of Dublin. The improved state of the RSTA finances meant that the lunch was provided from Central funds and that the Dublin members travelled from Heuston Station on the 11.00.am train and returned from Galway on the 6.05.pm. train.

The meeting itself would appear to have been lively with a proposal from Ms. Mary McCann, seconded by Ms. E. Cole, to raise the annual subscription to £5.00. After some discussion it was agreed to raise it to £4.00. The recommendation, which had come from the sub-committee established under Motion 293 of the ASTI Annual Convention of 1982, was discussed. The sub-committee had recommended the creation of a new form of ASTI membership, which would enable retired teachers to maintain contact with their serving colleagues. The term "Emeritus Membership" was to be used, and would be available to paid-up members of the ASTI when they retired. Emeritus members would have the right to attend and vote at Branch meetings of the ASTI and to attend Annual Convention as delegates but could not be members of the Central Executive Council or hold office in the ASTI.[41] Two former Presidents who attended the AGM had differing views on the proposal. Mr. Patrick Finnegan said the idea was to open up membership to retired teachers and that it could lead to a better negotiating position for the RSTA. Mr. George Lyons felt that the RSTA could cease to have any relevance and might lose its identity. It was decided to leave the matter in abeyance and to return to it at a further meeting. Dónal Ó'Conalláin was re-elected President and most of the outgoing committee members were returned to office.

It was noted that after the meeting the members were entertained in the bar by the Galway members and that Mr. Paddy Boyle, Editor of ASTIR, welcomed them both formally and informally and that the President replied suitably to their wonderful hospitality.[42]

No sooner had the committee members returned from Galway than they set about organising the Annual Dinner for October. In the meantime they received an invitation from the National Association of Pensioners and Pensioners' Associations (NAPPA) to join them. After some discussion and on the suggestion of Cathal O'Gara it was decided not to respond to the invitation as it was felt that no advantage would accrue to the RSTA.[43] Mr. Tomás Ó'Rian, no doubt remembering the visit to Galway suggested that the members should have an informal get-together occasionally. The spirit of bonhomie was evident when it was decided to invite the President, General Secretary and Honorary Treasurer of the ASTI to the Annual Dinner.

While the RSTA and the ASTI continued to have very cordial relations at that time there were tensions building up between some members of the RSTA and the official attitude of the ASTI to what was to become known as the Eileen Flynn case. Ms. Flynn was a secondary school teacher who had been dismissed from her school in New Ross in 1982 for a life-style that was alleged to be contrary to Catholic morals. She had become pregnant while living with a separated man. She had never been a member of the ASTI but she took her case to an employment appeals tribunal in 1983, which ruled against her in early 1984. She subsequently took her case to the Circuit Court and later to the High Court, which ruled against her.

Attitudes to Flynn within the ASTI were divided. Some felt that as she had never been a member that the union should stay out of the proceedings but younger members and those in Wexford felt that some support should be given to her. Kieran Mulvey, General Secretary of the ASTI wrote a strongly worded article in the Sunday Independent (February 12th 1984) defending the right of teachers to a private life. He was constrained in defending Flynn insofar as she was not a member but he called for a review and overhaul of Employment Equality and Unfair Dismissals legislation.

The ASTI Annual Convention in 1984 adopted a resolution that a teacher's private morality and lifestyle should not be grounds for dismissal where they conflict with the views of school management. This policy was not acceptable to all members of the ASTI, nor was it greeted with enthusiasm by some members of the RSTA. The matter came to a head at the Annual General Meeting of the RSTA in March 1985. That month's issue of ASTIR had contained a statement on the Eileen Flynn appeal judgement in which ASTI policy as decided at the previous year's Convention was re-iterated. Sally O'Halloran who had acted as informal secretary to the nascent Galway branch indicated that she wished to resign her duties and would no longer be available to distribute ASTIR to the Galway members. At an earlier meeting (January 9th 1985) she had said that Kitty Burke no longer wished to remain a member of the RSTA and that she had requested that no literature from the RSTA should be sent to her in future.

At the AGM the dismissal of Eileen Flynn was raised in a letter from Galway. Unfortunately the letter is not extant and its contents can only be gleaned from the recorded minutes of the meeting. The minutes report that some Galway members were unhappy with the stand taken by the ASTI in the matter and that Nora Kelleher and Patrick Finnegan spoke on the subject and that the meeting agreed that the RSTA had no call to intervene. A motion proposed by Robert Scanlan "that we endorse the statement from the Standing Committee as published in the March edition or ASTIR" was heavily defeated.[44]

The attitude of the RSTA was no different from that of many members of the ASTI. The membership was composed of elderly people who had grown up and worked in an era where strict public adherence to sexual morality was obligatory. Many of the older men would have been ex-seminarians and some were members of organisations such as Vexilia Regis or the Knights of Columbanus. The women members would have been greatly influenced by the ethos of the mainly convent schools in which they had taught and would have been shocked by what they considered to have been a public display of immorality.

The autumn of 1985 was to see a vigorous campaign of industrial action undertaken by the three main teacher unions under the banner of Teachers United. The campaign was undertaken because of the refusal of the Government to pay a pay increase that had been awarded after lengthy arbitration. This was something unprecedented in the history of Irish teacher unions and led to a massive campaign of industrial action in all sections of Irish primary and post-primary education. A series of rolling strikes was held throughout the country and it was proposed to have a mass meeting of striking teachers in Croke Park on December 5th 1985. An invitation to attend the rally was extended to the officers of the RSTA but none was available to attend.[45] The non-attendance of any officer of the RSTA at the Croke Park rally, at which 20,000 teachers participated, did not lessen the growing bonds between the RSTA and the ASTI. At a committee meeting of the RSTA on January 29th 1986 it was noted that an invitation had been received from the ASTI to send a representative to the ASTI Annual Conference in Bundoran. It was unanimously agreed that Dónal Ó'Conalláin should be the representative and it was noted that it would be the 50th Annual Convention that he had attended.

At the next committee meeting of the RSTA, held on April 9th 1986, Ó'Conalláin said that he had been treated with great hospitality when he attended his 50th Annual Convention. He reported that he had been wined and dined and presented with a silver salver and even had his hotel bill paid. He said it was gratifying to know that his services to the ASTI had been thus acknowledged.

The era of Ó'Conalláin's Presidency saw a great increase in the social activities of the RSTA. It was during his time that the Annual Dinner was established and the Annual General Meeting was also held in conjunction with a lunch. Monthly coffee mornings were held in Dublin and the RSTA notes printed in the ASTIR made frequent reference to social gatherings and there were frequent trips to destinations outside Dublin. While the overall membership seemed to hover around eighty, there was a definite move to spread the organisation outside the Dublin region. Ó'Conalláin's notes in ASTIR were always pithy and amusing with frequent references to the brighter side of life. They display little of the despair and frustration that was always present in the earlier records of the RSTA. This, of course, would have been helped in no small way by the granting of pension parity in the early eighties and also by the availability of free travel for those over sixty-six.

There is evidence of Ó'Conalláin's wry humour in many of his notes. In one he reflected on the ASTI policy of seeking full pension after thirty year's service and the possible consequences if such a desirable goal were to be achieved. He wondered aloud as to whether the ASTI had given sufficient consideration to the impact a mass-retirement would pose for the ASTI. He was happy to let the ASTI work out its own salvation but the RSTA would surely be a major beneficiary. He went on to say

"Imagine the invigorating influence of the influx of a horde of comparative youngsters to our ranks. By virtue of our numerical strength we would be courted by insurance brokers, investment agencies, tour operators and the like, offering hitherto undreamt of concessions in which we might all share. No doubt our neophytes, seeing their senior colleagues enjoying buckshee travel would soon inaugurate a campaign to have the free travel concession made applicable to all pensioners irrespective of age. Very understandable, seeing that some of them would have to wait 15 years under present regulations. All in all, the prospect is so exciting that one is tempted to hope that the policy now adopted will meet with early implementation." [46]

Ó'Conalláin had seen it all. He, with others such as Cathal O'Gara, Dan Buckley and Tadhg McCurtain, had fought for many years for what had only recently been achieved and he no doubt felt entitled to pen the slightly tongue-in-cheek article. Some years later a partial early retirement scheme was introduced but the granting of full pension after thirty years service now seem further away than at any time since the introduction of the Secondary Teachers' Pension Scheme in 1929.

The 1986 AGM was held in the Glentworth Hotel in Limerick, where the arrangements had been made by Ms. Kathleen O'Sullivan. O'Sullivan was the local representative of ASTI on Standing Committee. In the following year the AGM was held in the Shamrock Lodge Hotel, Athlone, where members of the Athlone Branch of the ASTI met the RSTA delegates at the railway station. Here again, they were facilitated by a local ASTI member, Ms. Teresa Kennedy. John White, President of the ASTI, attended. At this meeting Ó'Conalláin indicated his intention to resign from the office of President but he was persuaded to remain on. There was some discussion as to how they could increase membership and encourage more of the eighty eight paid up members to attend the AGM or the Annual Dinner. It was proposed that George Lyons, former President of the ASTI and lately resident in Galway and Queenie Clohessy of Tipperary should be co-opted to the national committee to better represent members outside of Dublin. This proposal was adopted unanimously. It was also agreed that the RSTA should produce a membership card, which might enable members to get a better rate in golf clubs etc. Dónal Ó'Conalláin and Cathal O'Gara were re-appointed as representatives on the JCCRSS.[47] Ó'Conalláin had been in failing health but he persisted to represent the interests of the RSTA with quiet good humour up to the time of his death in December 1987.

The last committee meeting chaired by Ó'Conalláin was held in the Royal Dublin Hotel on September 16th 1987 at which it was agreed that the usual guests would be invited to the Annual Dinner to be held in Buswell's Hotel, Dublin. It was also agreed that the Vice-President, Mona Hughes would seek special rates for any members wishing to stay overnight in the hotel.

One of the more significant matters to arise at that meeting was a letter from Michael Turner who had recently retired as headmaster of Templeogue College who expressed a wish to join the RSTA. Turner had been a very active member of the ASTI prior to his taking up the position in Templeogue College but he had resigned from the ASTI because of a possible conflict of interest. This was at a time when being Principal of a school was not compatible with ASTI membership. That situation had only recently been resolved by the acceptance of Boards of Management in voluntary secondary schools in 1985. In the event Turner was accepted into the RSTA and in future years he was to become one of its more prominent and effective members.

With the demise of Dónal Ó'Conalláin, Mona Hughes was elected President at the Annual General Meeting of April 28th 1988. George Lyons was elected Vice-President and reported to the meeting that he had been well received as the RSTA representative at the ASTI Annual Convention and that he had received a cheque for £500.00 from the ASTI, which he was now formally handing to the RSTA Honorary Treasurer, Willie Hanly.

Despite the subvention from the ASTI the finances of the RSTA gave cause for concern. Reporting to a committee meeting on January 18th 1989 the then treasurer said that the bank balance had fallen from £614.00 in December 1987 to £309.00. in December 1988. This was mainly due to the subsidies provided for the Annual Dinner, Annual Lunch and/or committee lunches. These subsidies would have to be reduced or the membership fee increased. A motion was proposed by Dan Buckley and seconded by Nora Kelleher, both former presidents of the ASTI, "That the subscription for members should not be increased," was defeated by five votes to four. As no positive motion was proposed it was decided that the committee would not make any specific recommendation to the Annual General Meeting.

The Annual General Meeting was held in the Newpark Hotel, Kilkenny, and attracted 35 members. Following the treasurer's report a discussion on the finances of the RSTA took place. On the proposal of Frank Campbell, seconded by Moira McDowell it was agreed to raise the annual subscription to £5.00. It reported that the membership had remained fairly static at around eighty members and various suggestions were made s to how membership could be increased. Previous attempts to get lists of retired members either from the Department of Education or the ASTI had been unsuccessful and it was now proposed that school stewards should be asked to give information to retiring teachers about the existence of the RSTA.

Under any other business the Honorary Secretary, Anna Rigney reported that she had in her private capacity attended a seminar in Dún Laoghaire organised by the Council for the Aged It dealt with the many problems of pensioners from all walks of life. She also reported that the National Federation of Pensioners Associations was anxious that the RSTA should join them. The meeting agreed that it would be desirable that the RSTA join the National Federation provided that membership would not run counter to the interests of the Joint Consultative Council with which the RSTA had a long association and on whose committee the RSTA had two representatives.

IN 1989 there was a hope that there would be an increase in membership of the RSTA due to the early retirement programme, which had been introduced during the previous year. In January 1988 the ASTI General Secretary, Kieran Mulvey had reported to the Standing Committee that copies of an early retirement scheme had been distributed to schools and that copies were available to members of Standing Committee. He, said that it was anticipated that between 200 and 300 teachers in secondary schools would be offered early retirement with the benefit of added years. At the next meeting of the Standing Committee on February 27th 1988 he reported that 304 secondary teachers had applied for the early retirement scheme. There is no record in the Standing Committee minutes of how many teachers actually retired but the expected large increase in RSTA members did not materialise. At the AGM on April 25th 1990 the outgoing President, Mona Hughes stated that membership had increased from 80 to 93. The minutes record that there was an attendance of around 40 who enjoyed a pleasant lunch but there is some evidence that not everyone was happy with what was being achieved for pensioners. James McSweeney raised the issue and was assured by the Chair that the matter of pensions was ". . . safely in the hands of the Joint Consultative Council of Retired State Servants and the National Federation of Pensioners' Associations. Also, since December 1990, retired teachers have [gained] a new ally to promote all their interests when the Retired Workers Committee of the Irish Congress of Trade Unions held its inaugural meeting at which the ASTI has a representation."[48] It is interesting to note that at the ASTI Standing Committee meeting on August 30th 1991 it was decided to refer an invitation to the Retired Workers' Committee meeting to the RSTA. Since that time two nominees to that committee have been proposed by the RSTA and ratified by the ASTI each year.

It is clear that McSweeney was not happy with the assurances given. On April 29th 1990 he wrote to the Honorary Secretary, Frank Campbell, submitting the following resolution for consideration by the committee: "[That] the committee of RSTI (sic) investigate ways and means of improving pension allowance and exemption from taxation of a certain percentage of pensions. That the committee report to members on progress within six months."

This was the first time in a number of years that discussion had arisen on the amount or the taxation of pensions. Ever since the revival of the RSTA in 1981 the principal activities of the association had been social with an emphasis on the Annual Dinner, lunch and coffee mornings with the annual Mass for deceased members, which was usually celebrated in St. Kevin's Oratory at the Pro Cathedral in Dublin. McSweeney's intervention seemed to herald a new development in the RSTA, which was to become more apparent later in the decade.

How much it influenced Mona Hughes to resign as President of the RSTA is unclear but at the 1990 AGM she announced that "she wished to be relieved of the burden of office." Glowing tributes were paid to her work on behalf of the association and it was stated that she was a worthy successor to the late Dónal Ó'Conalláin whose act was a difficult one to follow. George Lyons was elected president and the meeting ended with a presentation by a representative of Allied Irish Banks who addressed them on how to invest their savings. The Honorary Secretary, Frank Campbell made a rueful comment in the minutes when he recorded that

All seemed impressed with the sophistication of modern financial services. One has a great variety of investment options for any superfluous liquid assets, provided you have got it you can dabble in managed funds, unit trusts, dividend rich debentures. The message was reassuring but I left reminding myself of a possible snag: You've got to have money in the bank, Frank."

McSweeney's letter was dealt with at the next meeting of the RSTA Committee on June 20th 1990. The newly elected President, George Lyons, who was a former President and treasurer of the ASTI pointed out that the RSTA would have no standing on its own in making representations to the official side on the matters referred to in McSweeney's letter. They could only be processed through the Joint Consultative Council of Retired State Servants with possible assistance from the National Federation of Pensioners' Associations. The meeting proceeded to make arrangements for the Annual Dinner, to be held in Buswell's Hotel on Friday October 7th. It was noted that after a few unhappy experiences in Buswell's over meals there was a marked improvement in the quality of food and service at the AGM in April. Unfortunately George Lyons had died before the Annual Dinner.

George Lyons was a native of Hollymount, Co. Mayo and had taught in St. Joseph's CBS, Fairview, for most of his teaching career. When he retired he went to live in Headford, Co. Galway. He was a very active ASTI member and served as Treasurer and president. Writing in ASTIR in September 1990, Joe Costello said "I remember him as a distinguished and courteous man and a man of integrity and enlightened views. His Presidential Address in 1963 is still regarded as one of the most memorable ever."

After the demise of George Lyons, Maureen Gavan Duffy, who had been Vice President of the RSTA assumed the role of acting President and was confirmed in the role of President at the 1991 Annual General meeting, which was held in the Sacre Coer Hotel, Salthill, Galway on April 24th. It would appear that the social activities were very much to the fore at the meeting. Much of the recorded discussion concerned the selection of venues for the Annual Dinner and the following year's Annual General Meeting, with a suggestion that it be held in Cork. The spirit of James McSweeney lived on with a question from Patrick Finnegan as to whether the 1990 Arbitration award to teachers would be passed on to pensioners. He was told by the Honorary Secretary, Frank Campbell, that it would and that that had been made clear in an article in ASTIR in January 1991. Frank Campbell, because of illness, resigned as Honorary Secretary later that year but continued as a member of the committee. At a committee meeting in June 1991 the Honorary Treasurer, Willie Hanly reported that the finances stood at £1,325.00 due to an increased subvention of £800 per annum from the ASTI. The RSTA agreed to affiliate to the National Federation of Pensioners' Associations in November 1991.[49]

There is further evidence that the RSTA began to take a greater interest in likeminded organisations at that time. During the 1985/86 teachers' campaign a close bond had developed between the members of the three main teacher unions, ASTI, INTO and TUI. This group acted jointly as Teachers United.[50] At the conclusion of that campaign it was felt that some form of federation might be the best way forward for teachers. As a result a Council of Teachers' Unions was formed with Mr. Eoin de Buitléir acting as administrative officer. De Buitléir proposed a series of pre-retirement courses for teachers and wrote to the RSTA to apprise them of his intentions. One of the committee members, Bríd Hanrahan offered to speak at any such course that would be held.[51]

In August 1991 the ASTI, as already noted, received a letter from the Irish Congress of Trade Unions informing them of a proposed meeting of the newly formed Retired Workers Committee to be held on October 11th.[52] It was decided to refer the letter to the RSTA and the Honorary Secretary Ms. Maeve Colbert was the first representative of the RSTA to attend a meeting of that body in Parnell Square on 25th November 1991.[53] She had also been invited to lunch with members of the Retired Teachers Association of the TUI and attended on of their committee meetings.[54] She said that the TUI members were interested in the concept of coffee mornings, which had long been a feature of the RSTA but was mostly observed in Dublin. She also attended further meetings of the Retired Workers Committee of the ICTU and a seminar organised by that body in Dundalk.

The early nineties were the years when the RSTA began to break out from the usual routine of coffee mornings and annual dinners and lunches and to seek further association with other kindred bodies. Admittedly the RSTA had had considerable involvement with the Joint Consultative Council of Retired State Servants since the very foundation of the association. George Lodge and the early officers of the

RSTA frequently referred to the importance of that connection but as the terms and conditions of pensioners had improved the social dimension increased. While the RSTA still numbered less than a hundred members it began to spread its wings and Maeve Colbert, as Honorary Secretary, played a not inconsiderable part in that broadening of the horizons. She attended the launching by the Taoiseach of "1993 The European Year of Older People and Solidarity between Generations" at Dublin Castle.[55] She had also involved RSTA members in a tree planting initiative called "Coill na nOidí," which provided a wider profile for the RSTA. Máirín Flynn attended a seminar on November 4th and 5th 1994 for the purpose of establishing a Senior Citizens' Parliament.[56]

In 1995 the Honorary Secretary was able to report that membership then numbered 109 paid up members but that most of them were Dublin based. Despite the efforts of the officers over more than thirty years there had been little expansion outside the capital. There had been some very active members in places such as Galway, Cork, Kilkenny and Kerry but the main locus of activity was still Dublin. It was in this context that proposals emerged for the re-structuring of the RSTA as a branch of the Association of Secondary Teachers, Ireland.

CHAPTER 4:
EMERITUS MEMBERSHIP OF THE ASTI

The concept of Emeritus membership of the ASTI arose from a motion that was adopted at the Annual Convention at the Talbot Hotel, Wexford in April 1982.

Motion 293, from the Galway Branch, proposed: "That Convention decides in principle that retired teachers who were members of the ASTI should retain their links with the ASTI as full or associate members or through some other form of membership which would entitle them to the services of the ASTI on their behalf." A second part of the motion proposed that a sub-committee be set up to recommend how the decision should be implemented and that it should report its findings to the Christmas meeting of the CEC.[57] It was a particularly apposite motion presented to annual convention twenty years after the formation of the Retired Secondary Teachers' Association in 1962.

The sub-committee reported on how the spirit of the resolution could be implemented and made recommendations on the rule changes that would be required. The sub-committee recommended to the CEC "That all eligible retired teachers be accorded the opportunity to become Emeritus members" and that a new Rule should be inserted in the constitution of the ASTI establishing the conditions and entitlements of Emeritus members. It was agreed that Emeritus members should have the rights and privileges of full members with the exception that they could not act as Branch officers or as representatives on the CEC. Nor could they vote on industrial action, be candidates for trusteeship of the association or receive benefit from the Sickness Benefit or Benevolent funds. It was silent on the matter of eligibility to be a branch delegate to annual or special conventions. It did recommend that the subscription payable by Emeritus members should be determined under Rule 125. In the event the Honorary National Treasurer never sought to impose a membership fee and custom and practice has been that no annual membership fee has been paid to the ASTI and the role of Emeritus membership has been seen as an honour bestowed on retired members. The decision to create a category of Emeritus membership was very far-sighted and was unique within the trade union movement. Until this, the concept of the emeritus role had generally been confined to higher academic institutions, where professors who had retired were often referred to as emeritus professors. There can be little doubt but that the proponents of the scheme in the ASTI were conscious of the professional implications of the motion but it also enabled retired members of the ASTI to keep in contact with their former colleagues who were still teaching. It also provided a continuing transfer of information from an older to a younger generation of teachers.

The Retired Secondary Teachers' Association welcomed the new development and encouraged intending retirees to apply for emeritus membership through their union branches. Not all retirees availed of the privilege but some of the more active members of the ASTI did and continued to attend their branch meetings and sometimes went to Annual Convention as delegates.

In the mid 1990s the Executive Council of the Irish Congress of Trade Unions commissioned a report on the status of retired workers in the trade union movement. The report was commissioned because it was felt that in some instances the trade union movement paid little attention to the welfare of its retired members. Introducing the report to the ICTU Biennial Conference in 1995, Michael O'Halloran said that after forty years of membership of a trade union there was still a need for a person to have a link with his or her trade union. He said that good work had already been done in that area by some unions but that he would urge every union to establish a retired workers committee and that every union should nominate a representative to the Retired Workers' Committee. Only twenty-four of the sixty-six unions had responded to a questionnaire on the status of retired workers and only three of these had full participation for retired workers. It was obvious that the ASTI was well to the fore in the trade union movement in regard to its attitude to its retired members who had the benefit of membership of the Retired Secondary Teachers' Association and also the right to become emeritus members of the ASTI.

The main recommendations of the Report on the Status of Retired Workers in the Trade Union Movement were incorporated in Motion 63,[58] which was adopted by the Biennial conference. A further motion (Motion J) to amend the constitution of the ICTU so that the objects of congress should also apply to retired members was also adopted.

At an ASTI Standing Committee meeting held on 27th January 1995 a series of draft proposals in relation to retired and emeritus members was presented.[59] It was stated that at that time there were forty-four emeritus members and that retired members could also become members of the Retired Secondary Teachers' Association. It was also stated that that body was relatively small and that it did not have administrative resources to organise effectively. It was further stated that there was an ongoing debate in the trade union movement as to how unions could best provide facilities for members. The proposals, inter alia, were that the ASTI should establish a single national branch for retired members, that a small monthly subscription should be remitted to the ASTI for administrative costs and that an official in Head Office would be assigned responsibility for the branch. These were essentially draft proposals and it was agreed that the involvement of members of the proposed branch in Standing Committee elections and the relationship of the branch to Standing Committee regions would have to be decided. Participation of members in ASTI Conventions and in CEC and other offices of the union would also have to be decided. There is no record of the role of emeritus members being discussed. It was agreed that consultation with the RSTA should take place and it was later reported that at a subsequent meeting Mr. Frank Campbell on behalf of the RSTA welcomed the proposals. The report was adopted without debate at the ASTI convention in 1995. It was the second last item on a long agenda, which for three days had been very concerned about possible industrial action in relation to proposals on early retirement.

Proposals for the organisation of a Retired Secondary Teachers Association Branch were included in Motion 164 for the Annual Convention in 1996. The motion was comprehensive and complex, extending over six pages of the Convention Handbook and involving many rule changes.[60] The proposed branch would elect two members to act as delegates and two members to act as observers to the ASTI Annual Convention. The branch would be entitled to submit a report to Annual Convention but would not be permitted to submit motions, nor to vote on national ballots or in matters pertaining to the salaries, rights and conditions of other ASTI members. Neither would it be permitted to vote in elections for CEC, Standing Committee or union office except in the case of the two delegates to Annual Convention. This would represent a severe curtailment on the rights and entitlements of Emeritus members under the existing rules but even more restrictive was the proposal to amend Rule 14 of the constitution by addition of "with effect from the end of Annual Convention 1996 access to Emeritus Membership shall cease. Entitlement to Emeritus Membership shall continue for those who currently hold Emeritus Membership status."[61]

In the event no decisions were taken by the ASTI in the 1990s on the controversial issues of emeritus membership and the establishment of a single RSTA branch. The RSTA continued on its independent course, after the tensions of the mid-nineties eased and cordial relations were resumed with the parent body. The ASTI continued to subvent the RSTA and in a spirit of goodwill donated a computer to the organisation. The ASTI also agreed to post copies of ASTIR to all RSTA members as well as an annual diary. The ASTI assigned the nomination of its two delegates to the Retired Workers committee of the Irish Congress of Trade Unions to the National Executive of the RSTA. In many ways it could be said that the RSTA enjoyed a better relationship with its parent union than other retired workers enjoyed with their erstwhile unions.

Members of the RSTA were surprised when a motion concerning emeritus membership appeared on the agenda for the ASTI Annual convention in 2011. The motion proposed a change to Rule 14(b) of the Rules of the ASTI. Rule 14 is the rule, which states the conditions under which retired teachers who were members of the ASTI at their retirement may become emeritus members. Sub-section (b) while stating that emeritus members shall have the power to exercise all of the rights and privileges of full members lists a number of limitations to these privileges. Emeritus members may not act as Branch Officers or as representatives on the Central Executive Council or contest any election for trusteeship of the ASTI. Nor can they vote in any ballot for industrial action. Notwithstanding these restrictions the presence of Emeritus members at branch meetings of the ASTI and as delegates to ASTI Annual Conventions had been increasing over the years. This may have been related in some measure to the RSTA encouraging retirees to seek emeritus membership.

The amendment proposed under Motion 89 would see further restrictions placed on the entitlements of emeritus members. If the motion were adopted it would mean that emeritus members could no longer attend ASTI Convention as branch delegates nor would they be entitled to be members of any committee or sub-committee of the ASTI. These proposals caused some alarm in the RSTA as some members had been active participants in some sub-committees of the ASTI, most notably the Pensions sub-committee. The possibility that the motion would be adopted by convention prompted a large attendance of emeritus members as delegates to the 2011 Annual Convention. They were prepared to argue their case for the retention of the right to attend conventions and to seek to be elected to sub-committees of the ASTI. In the event they did not get an opportunity to present their case. On the proposal of a procedural motion Convention agreed that Motion 89 should be referred to the Review Committee on ASTI Structures. At a meeting between ASTI and RSTA officers subsequent to the withdrawal of the motion, clarification was sought as to the possible future of emeritus membership. The RSTA representatives were assured that the matter would be dealt with in a report being compiled by Genesis, a management consultancy firm, which had been commissioned to conduct a review of ASTI structures and organisation. That report would be presented to a Special Convention of the ASTI. At the time of writing that report has not yet been presented and the future role of emeritus members in the ASTI is undecided.

CHAPTER 5:
PROPOSALS FOR A RETIRED SECONDARY TEACHERS' BRANCH OF THE ASTI

In 1992 the RSTA had been in existence for thirty years. It was mainly Dublin based and as most of the aims in relation to pensions had been achieved it was more concerned with social activities than with agitation for improved rights for retired members. A symbiotic relationship had developed with the ASTI, which continued to subvent the organisation and to be generally supportive.

Attempts to expand beyond the Dublin region had been less than successful although some Annual General Meetings had been held outside the capital. No definite plan had emerged as to how the RSTA might expand in the future. Meanwhile, changes had been occurring within the ASTI.

In 1991 Charlie Lennon succeeded Kieran Mulvey as General Secretary of the ASTI. Lennon, who had worked for the INTO, had been appointed assistant general secretary of the ASTI in 1988 and when Kieran Mulvey retired to take up a position as Chairman of the Labour Relations Commission in 1991 Lennon was appointed General Secretary. While neither Mulvey or Lennon had previous experience in the ASTI before their appointments to senior positions within the union they differed greatly in their approach to problems. Mulvey was very upfront and has been described as gregarious and outgoing. He had once been a student activist and had retained a lot of the bravura associated with that role. He had a very easy manner even with those with whom he vehemently disagreed. Lennon, on the other hand, was probably a more cautious administrator and less of the "hail fellow well met." He was generally very well regarded among his fellow trade union officials within the Irish Congress of Trade unions but he was less engaging with the members of the RSTA than Mulvey. When Mulvey had taken over from the previous General Secretary, Máire MacDonagh in 1983 he was taking over an organisation, which was run by the members for the members. It still exhibited many of the qualities that had been responsible for its formation and evolution. MacDonagh had acted as more of a secretary who carried out the decisions of the executive in a very close collaborative manner with the President and the Standing Committee. If leadership roles were to be defined as being either in the mould of chairman or chief it would be wrong to define MacDonagh in either role. The President tended to combine both roles but was very ably supported by the General Secretary, who was a very formidable negotiator. Mulvey was the transition person. He made contact with the grass roots and showed his strength during the Teachers United Campaign of 1985-86. In many ways the appointment of Lennon as assistant General Secretary in 1988 backed up the flamboyant nature of Mulvey's character with the more introspective administrative abilities of Lennon. After Lennon was appointed General Secretary in 1991 he initiated a series of changes in the administration of the ASTI. Some of the structures within the ASTI had long been deemed to be cumbersome and unwieldy. The most notable example was the Central Executive Council, which at that time consisted of approximately one hundred and fifty members. It was the second most important decision making body in the union and met at least twice a year but in times of crisis, much more frequently. Numerous attempts, down through the years, had been made to either abolish it or to reduce its size but all attempts at change had been resisted by the members. The day to day affairs of the ASTI were decided by the Standing Committee of fifteen members who were elected nationally at the Annual Convention. There was a feeling that some parts of the country were better represented on the committee than others.

At the 1992 Annual Convention, held in Tralee, a motion was adopted which accepted in principle that Standing Committee should be elected on a regional basis and a sub-committee was established to draw up procedures for the implementation of the decision. That sub-committee made a detailed report to the Central Executive Council in January 1993 outlining how the proposed regionalisation would be implemented and amended proposals were adopted at a Special Convention held in Galway on April 16th 1993. The regionalisation of the Standing Committee increased the membership from fifteen to twenty three but did nothing to lessen the influence of the larger Central Executive Council. The regionalisation of the Standing Committee had brought the internal ASTI structures more in line with those which obtained in the INTO, with which Lennon would have had some considerable experience.

At several meetings between November 1994 and April 1995 the Standing Committee of the ASTI addressed the position of retired secondary teachers and their relationship with the ASTI. These discussions were not initiated by the RSTA but appear to have come from officials within the ASTI Head Office and were monitored by Pat King, a former Honorary National Organiser, later to become General Secretary of the ASTI. The proposals that emerged were that the RSTA should be reconstituted as a branch of the ASTI. This was similar to the relationship which existed within the INTO and some other unions. The proposals were discussed with the President of the RSTA, Mr. Frank Campbell, who reported on them to a meeting of the RSTA on January 18th 1995. He told the meeting that it had been intimated to him that the proposals would raise the status of the RSTA but the members present at the meeting indicated that they thought "the status quo should remain."[62]

This was the first indication of a difference of opinion between the RSTA and the Standing Committee of the ASTI on this matter. At a meeting of Sub-Committee C of the ASTI Standing Committee, held on January 27th 1995, it was reported that a meeting had been held with Mr. Frank Campbell on the draft proposals for continued membership for retired ASTI members and that he had welcomed the proposals and the enhanced service they would bring for retired members. It seems clear that the Standing Committee had no knowledge of the decision of the RSTA committee on January 18th to retain the status quo. In the event, the Standing Committee decided to proceed with the establishment of an RSTA branch and to analyse more deeply the costs involved in running the branch, the benefits and rights of the member and the exclusions that might apply. The fact that the sub-committee was to be charged with examining what exclusions would apply to members of the proposed branch was a clear indication that they were not to be regarded in the same light as members of an ordinary branch.

The draft proposals for the formation of a Retired Second-Level Teachers' Association (sic) were included in the Honorary National Organiser's Report to the ASTI Annual Convention in 1995 and were thus deemed to be policy. The matter was not debated or discussed at Convention but was formally adopted, as were many other reports.[63] This was essentially a working document and was to undergo many changes in the following eighteen months.

At the AGM of the RSTA, held at the Newpark Hotel, Kilkenny, on April 26th 1995, copies of the draft proposals from the ASTI for the establishment of a Retired Secondary Teachers' Branch were distributed to the delegates and a decision was made to send copies to those members who were not present. It was agreed on the proposal of Peter Kerr, seconded by Máirín O'Flynn, that the document should be accepted as a working document and that the committee would take submissions from members when they had studied it. The proposals as presented extended to three A4 typed pages. It was apparent that the proposed branch would have very limited powers as compared to full membership, which would reflect the reduced annual subscription of £24.00 per annum (approximately 17% of the full membership fee that was applicable at that time).

The proposals were again discussed at a committee meeting of the RSTA on June 22nd 1995. Former President of the ASTI, Dan Buckley, said that he believed that the whole idea was impracticable and unrealistic and that the majority of retired teachers did not join the RSTA and were not interested in joining because of age or health problems. Peter Kerr agreed with Dan Buckley and felt that the plan was non-viable and was far too cumbersome and that further discussion with the ASTI would be necessary. Máirín O'Flynn, assistant Honorary Secretary RSTA, felt that the members should rise to the challenge that was presented and felt that it should be promoted on a regional basis and not just as a single branch. She also said that if early retirement was forthcoming that the branch structure could be quite successful. It was agreed that further negotiation was needed on the matter.

A delegation of nine members of the RSTA met with Charlie Lennon, Pat King and John Mulcahy, Vice-President of the ASTI on September 19th 1995. The background to the development of the position paper on "Retired Secondary Teachers" branch was explained to the RSTA delegation. It was stated that the intention of the proposals was to provide a professional and effective service for retired ASTI members and to provide them with a continued opportunity for ASTI involvement.[64]

The RSTA delegation expressed concerns with some aspects of the position paper, saying that it could have been presented in a more positive light and that more emphasis should have been placed on the benefits that might arise rather than the restrictions that might be imposed on members of the RSTA. The RSTA delegation stated that emeritus members, under existing arrangements could have full local involvement and could also attend Annual Convention as delegates and that it was now proposed to remove these entitlements. It was also noted that in the proposed branch structure RSTB members would only be permitted to attend Annual Convention as non-voting observers. The proposed annual subscription of £25.00 was also criticised as being too high for those who were not in receipt of a full salary whereas Emeritus Membership was free.

Following this meeting Pat King wrote to Frances Clarke, Honorary Secretary of the RSTA indicating changes that could be considered to the draft proposals. Among them was recognition that the proposed branch would be called the RSTA branch as distinct from the original proposal to name it RSTB. This ensured the continuity of the name. A concession was to be made by reducing the annual subscription from £25.00 to £20.00. It was also proposed that the emeritus membership should be retained for current emeritus members only and that the RSTA Branch would be permitted to elect two voting delegates and two observers to ASTI Annual Convention.[65]

These amended proposals were discussed at a committee meeting of RSTA on October 18th 1995. While the majority of the committee was in favour of the proposals it was decided that a letter should be sent to Pat King informing him of certain reservations which had been expressed at the meeting.[66] The reservations included the proposed subscription of £20.00 per annum. At that time the annual subscription to the RSTA was a mere £5.00 per year. There was also a worry as to what would happen to the £1,000.00 annual subvention which was being given to the RSTA at that time. On the administrative side a question was asked as to whether the RSTA would be permitted to propose motions in relation to retired members at Annual Convention and would emeritus members be able to retain such membership both at their previous branch and at the new RSTA branch level.

These queries were addressed by Pat King in a cordial reply to Frances Clarke.[67] In it he emphasised the intention that the ASTI would provide a comprehensive range of services and facilities for those who paid the RSTA subscription. He said that the branch would be funded by the return of a portion of the annual subscription and by further subvention from ASTI Head Office as required and that the subvention in the early years would be of the same order as that already in operation. He reiterated that while the RSTA branch would not be permitted to propose specific matters to Convention, it would be possible for the branch to communicate its views through the Annual Report to Convention. Recommendations in a report, once adopted by Convention, became ASTI policy. On the question of emeritus members retaining membership of two branches he stated that this would not be possible.

Within the ASTI the proposals for the formation of the Retired Secondary Teachers Branch were being monitored by Sub-Committee C of the Standing Committee, which was apprised of all developments by Pat King, Senior Official. As the negotiations were ongoing there were frequent amendments to the proposals. The sub-committee again examined the proposed Rule changes relating to the creation of the Retired Secondary Teachers' Association branch on Nov 17th 1995 and recommended their acceptance with a number of minor amendments in accordance with the discussions with the RSTA.[68] The way appeared to have been cleared for the establishment of the Retired Secondary Teachers' Association Branch and Pat King prepared details of the proposed Rule changes which would be necessary to inaugurate the new branch. These would have to be passed by the ASTI Annual Convention.

The proposals to establish a Retired Secondary Teachers' Association Branch were included in the agenda for 1996 ASTI Annual Convention under Motion 164.[69] This motion proposed no fewer than twenty changes to the Rules of the ASTI so as to accommodate the formation of the new branch. In the preamble to Motion 164 reference was made to a report adopted by the Irish Congress of Trade Unions at its 1995 Biennial Conference. This report urged each union to examine its rules and structures with a view to making necessary changes to provide for the participation of retired workers in the life of the union. In some ways the ASTI was ahead of other unions in the ICTU and had already begun to look at the role of the RSTA in advance of the recommendation of the ICTU. It was also stated in the preamble that the intention of the proposal was to provide retired teachers with an enhanced level of ASTI involvement and access to union facilities. It was further noted that all the proposals were contingent on each other and would have to be accepted in their entirety. In addition it was proposed that "With effect from the end of Annual Convention 1996 access to emeritus membership shall cease. Entitlement to emeritus membership shall continue for those who currently hold emeritus membership status."[70] The proposals envisaged a branch that would have a very restricted role within the ASTI and would not be comparable with other branches in its right to submit motions to Convention or to vote in elections to CEC or Standing Committee.

In the event, the proposals were not adopted at the 1996 Annual Convention. A great deal of time at the Convention was devoted to those aspects of the Programme for Competitiveness and Work (PCW), which concerned the pay and conditions of teachers and no time was available to debate the motion about the Retired Teachers branch, which was scheduled for Thursday April 11th.

The AGM of the RSTA was held on May 2nd 1996. There were two principal items of concern to the members. The first was an update on the PCW negotiations, which initially were not going to be of any benefit to retired teachers but would effectively have broken the parity with serving teachers. Attention had been drawn to this development at a previous committee meeting of the RSTA on March 30th,[71] at which a letter from Charlie Lennon to Peter Kerr was read in which he (Lennon) explained that no benefits would be forthcoming to retired teachers from the PCW package. The new package was deemed to be a restructuring of salary rather than a general increase across the board. Great disappointment was expressed at this meeting and it was proposed that a letter should be sent to Lennon in which it should be pointed out that the ASTI had a duty to look after the interests of retired teachers. The letter from Lennon had mentioned a possible pro-rata or ex-gratia payment for retired teachers in the future but it was felt that this was akin to the classic quotation of "live horse and you get grass." Peter Kerr had also sent letters to the national and provincial press in which he outlined his misgivings about the PCW.

By the time of the AGM on May 2nd there was evidence of increasing militancy within the ranks of the RSTA. At the outset draft standing orders had been adopted - hitherto meetings had been conducted on an informal basis. It was reported that committee members had attended meetings of the Federation of Pensioners and the Retired Workers' Pensioners Association to organise against the failure of the PCW to recognise the rights of retired workers. It was now believed that the Minister for Education was committed to including retired teachers in the new negotiations but it was not yet known what manner of benefit would be forthcoming. There was unanimous agreement among the 36 members present that parity should be maintained. It was decided that a deputation of four members, Peter Kerr, Michael Turner, Tadhg McCurtain and Margaret Stewart should meet the ASTI negotiators and that they should be told that the restructuring of salary in relation to productivity should not be allowed to interfere with indexing of pensions.

Pat King addressed the meeting and said that as the proposals to establish the RSTA branch had not been adopted at the Annual Convention they would be again on the agenda for the 1997 Convention. He went on to say that the formation of the new branch could lead to increased membership (at that time there were 117 paid up members of the RSTA and in time could lead to the formation of regional branches. He noted that most of the members were from Dublin while some counties had no members at all and that if a branch were formed there would be better service for retired teachers as the ASTI would be directly responsible for the branch. It must have been difficult to convince the members in view of their earlier attitude to the PCW negotiations. Peter Kerr remarked that if the proposals went ahead that the RSTA would have no voice at the ASTI Convention and that it would not be represented on committees. In reply Pat King said that the RSTA could submit an annual report to Convention and it might be possible to have a liaison officer speak on behalf of the RSTA. Dan Buckley said that the final decision on the matter would have to be made by the members and in the meantime negotiations would have to continue to ensure the best deal for retired members.

As predicted by Pat King, the proposals to establish a Retired Secondary Teachers' Association branch again appeared on the agenda for the Annual convention, 1997. In the meantime the ASTI had designated one of its senior officials, Mary McDonnell, to act as liaison officer with the RSTA, a development which was acknowledged at the RSTA AGM on April 17th 1997. At the AGM it was stated that "Mary is a most gracious individual who is always ready to deal with queries by phone or otherwise."[72] Yet again the pressure of business, in particular that associated with the Programme for Competitiveness and Work, prevented debate on the proposed Rule changes which would have allowed for the establishment of the RSTA branch. In accordance with Rule 66 (ii) of the ASTI the matter was referred to a Rules Convention to be held in Jury's Hotel, Ballsbridge, Dublin on may 17th 1997.

The motion to establish a Retired Secondary Teachers' branch was defeated at the Rules Convention in May. Seán Geraghty, who had represented the RSTA at the Convention, reported that the feeling of dissatisfaction with ASTI leadership was evident at the Convention. Margaret Stewart, Vice President asked that it be put on the record that relations between the RSTA and the ASTI were good and Michael Turner agreed that this was so and should remain the case.[73] He went on to say that they should endeavour to build up their membership and strengthen their Association.

CHAPTER 6:
THE PROGRAMME FOR COMPETITIVENESS AND WORK

From the time that the first proposals to establish a Retired Members' branch in the ASTI emerged there had been mixed feelings about the concept within the RSTA itself. The first proposals had been welcomed by the RSTA President, Frank Campbell, but as the proposals were developed they were not greeted with total unanimity.

From the mid-nineties there was a definite shift in the attitude of the RSTA from being a convivial social club to one that became very concerned with the possible threat to the pensions of its members. The principal reason for the switch in emphasis from social activities to direct pension issues can be attributed to the publication by the Government in February 1994 of the Programme for Competitiveness and Work. There had been two national wage agreements since the late 1980s and in each of them the wage increases granted to workers had in all cases been passed on to retired workers in the public service on a pro-rata basis. Pension parity had been the reason for the establishment of the RSTA in 1962 and had been the driving force of the organisation in its early years, until it was granted in 1973. Even then a time lag remained which was not resolved for some years. The Programme for Competitiveness and Work (PCW) was a much more complex agreement than the two previous ones and it was not envisaged that increases granted to workers would be passed on to those who were already retired. This was to be the submerged rock, which was to sink the proposals for the establishment of the Retired Secondary Teachers' Association Branch.

Negotiations on the PCW were lengthy and complex and in the case of teachers it involved the introduction of elements of productivity that had not existed beforehand. There were to be certain rewards for the introduction of these changes in work practices and an enhanced pension scheme with early retirement was to be introduced. As negotiations proceeded it became apparent that some allowances to be paid to serving teachers would not be paid to those who had already retired. It was two years after the publication of the initial PCW proposals before the RSTA adopted a formal position on the PCW, which was to lead to probably the most acrimonious period in the history of the RSTA.

The first indication of RSTA dissatisfaction with the PCW had occurred at a committee meeting on March 20th 1996 when Peter Kerr, Vice President had read a letter from the ASTI General Secretary, Charlie Lennon explaining that no benefits would accrue to pensioners from the PCW package. This was the start of a period of tension between the RSTA and the ASTI. At the AGM of the RSTA on May 2nd 1996 Frank Campbell resigned as President and was replaced by Peter Kerr, while Willie Hanly, who had been treasurer for 10 years also resigned and was replaced by Éilís Delaney. Peter Kerr had been a long time trade union activist and member of the Standing Committee with an involvement going back before the 1969 strike.

A meeting of the RSTA committee was held on May 19th 1996. The first item on the agenda was a discussion to determine the tactics to be adopted by the delegation, which had been chosen at the AGM to present the RSTA case at the proposed negotiations with the ASTI in relation to the PCW package. It was agreed that the delegation should emphasise the need to maintain parity with serving teachers.[74] It was also agreed that a very precise wording should be used and that arguments should be well formulated and that a decision should be made as to the tactics to be adopted. Tadhg McCrohan produced a two sheet memorandum outlining in detail the main points which should be emphasised and Michael Turner stressed that the main thing to be looked for was the preservation of the indexing of pensions. As a result of the discussion a ten-point plan was agreed which was to be presented to the ASTI negotiators on the PCW if and when such a meeting had been arranged.

It was further agreed that the delegation would ask the negotiators if it were acceptable to them that pensions should be excluded from the package and would they insist that the principle of the indexing of pensions be maintained. The RSTA was also concerned that restructuring was being tied to productivity and was worried that if this were to be the sole criterion for future salary increases what about the other determinants of increase i.e. inflation, increased general prosperity, established relativities etc. The RSTA was particularly concerned that past productivity was not considered and they instanced the fact that many retired teachers had taught 29-hour weeks with 40 plus pupils in a class. They had taught at a time when there was a longer teaching year with compulsory homework supervision and often arbitrary dismissal. They would ask if it were acceptable that their pensions should be depressed. It was clear that the attitude within the RSTA was reverting to what it had been thirty years earlier when George Lodge had constantly drawn attention to the failure to have proper indexing between current salaries and pensions.

At a committee meeting of the RSTA held on September 10th 1996 it was reported that a delegation from the RSTA had met with the ASTI negotiators on the PCW. They had been told that the Minister for Education had promised a raise of 3% across the board but that there was no way of ascertaining what this actually meant and how it would apply to retired teachers and particularly to the allowances which were promised in the PCW. It was noted that the negotiations were ongoing with regard to serving teachers and that their problems would have to be solved before any clarification would be made regarding pensioners. The RSTA committee decided to send a letter to the Minister for Education, Niamh Breathnach, asking her to meet a delegation from them and that a further letter should also be sent to the Minister for Finance regarding parity of pensions. There is no recorded evidence that either of these letters were sent at that time.

At the next meeting of the RSTA committee on Nov 18th 1996 it was noted that there would be no ballot on the PCW proposals by the ASTI members until the Nurse's Organisation (INO) had voted. It was also noted that there was growing dissatisfaction within many public service bodies with the pension arrangements in the PCW. A letter was received from Michael Turner outlining the losses to pensioners if parity was not retained. In it he pointed out that the ASTI had always regarded allowances as part of basic pay and quoted the ASTI Submission to the Department of Labour in 1980 in support of his argument. The meeting agreed to co-opt Michael Turner and James McSweeney to the committee. It was further agreed that an Extraordinary General Meeting of all members of the RSTA should be convened to set up an Action Committee to plan a campaign to retain parity and would seek support from other bodies, ASTI members and TDs.

The Extraordinary General Meeting was held in the Teachers' Club, Parnell Square on December 5ᵗʰ 1996. There was a large attendance with many travelling from outside Dublin. There was a surprise visit from John White, Deputy General Secretary of the ASTI and John Hurley, Vice President of the ASTI who arrived to explain the difficulties encountered in pursuing traditional parity. They pointed out that a given percentage across the board might be a better deal than traditional parity and while the allocation of 2% was rejected it was felt that a higher percentage of between 5% and 6% might be achieved. They said that the ASTI was endeavouring to secure the maximum benefits for all retired teachers. This view was also expressed in a letter from Charlie Lennon, which was read at the meeting, in which he stressed that the ASTI had always supported parity and would continue to do so but that there was a difficulty in applying parity as such to the PCW package because of the emphasis on restructuring.

After some considerable discussion it was decided "That an action committee be set up to extend and coordinate the RSTA campaign to copper fasten the principle of parity in relation to the PCW package and all future negotiations concerning increases in the remuneration of secondary teachers." The motion was adopted and an action committee was elected. The members were Peter Kerr, Michael Turner, Seán Geraghty, James McSweeney, Margaret Stewart, Tadhg McCrohan and Kevin Kilgarriff. The last three named were associated with the emerging Western Branch of the RSTA which was being promoted by Margaret Stewart in Galway, the other members were all Dublin based.

Members of the Action Group distributed leaflets to delegates attending the Central Executive Council of the ASTI on January 11ᵗʰ 1997. In the leaflet they stated that they did not seek to interfere with the rights of serving teachers and should they reject the PCW proposals they would accept it but if any proposals were to be accepted, which included increases in allowances for post holders, degree and diploma allowances and for those with ten years on the maximum point of the salary scale, that they should be passed on to retired teachers. It was stated that the RSTA was composed of teachers who had fought for justice in the past and they were now seeking the support of serving teachers to support their claim and ensure that traditional parity was not negated or diluted in the future. The leaflet concluded, "Justice must not be sacrificed upon the altar of expediency."[75]

The CEC decided by a vote of 78 to 77 to put revised proposals on the PCW to a ballot of members with a recommendation for acceptance.[76] In further clarification of the pensions issue the ASTI stated that proposals in relation to public service pension issues were being addressed through direct discussions between the Department of Finance and the ICTU and that "All of the public service unions, including the ASTI, are committed to maintaining their principle of parity between increases in pensions and salaries. There is no proposal to break that principle."[77]

It went on to state that not all benefits associated with the PCW would transfer to the pensions of retired teachers but that most pensioners would benefit from a percentage increase equal approximately to the value of the proposals for teacher in service. The object of the ASTI in this area is to maximise the benefits of the application of the deal to the maximum number of retired teachers."[78] The revised proposals were accepted by ASTI members by a vote of 63% to 37% but RSTA members continued to hope that progress could be made on the parity issue.

By the early months of 1997 a clear division was beginning to emerge within the ranks of the RSTA as to how the threat posed to existing pensions should be addressed by the ASTI. There was a section that was quite happy to participate in the social activities that had developed in the RSTA from the time that full pension parity had been established in 1973 and there was another group that had become increasingly aware of the threat to the whole concept of pension parity that was posed by the PCW. The latter group included Peter Kerr, Seán Geraghty, James McSweeney, Máirín O'Flynn and Michael Turner. They had all been long-time activists within the ASTI and were very aware of how such organisations worked.

Michael Turner had been a member of the ASTI since 1946. He was a loyal trade unionist and a gifted educationalist. He had written textbooks on Geography and Civics and contributed articles to Studies, The Furrow, Geographical Viewpoint, Education Studies and The Secondary Teacher. In 1977 he was appointed Principal of Templeogue College, Dublin and remained there until his retirement in 1987. He was one of the first lay people to be appointed Principal of a Catholic Voluntary Secondary School in Ireland, which in itself was an indication of the regard with which he was held notwithstanding his trade union activities.

During the early months of 1997 Turner produced a comprehensive dossier of facts and figures amounting to 48 pages of meticulously prepared typescript in support of his arguments against the acceptance of the PCW proposals in regard to teachers' pensions. These arguments or excerpts based on them were used to lobby the officers of the ASTI and members of the Central Executive Council and Standing Committee. He was very critical of the concept of productivity as it was to be applied to secondary school teachers. In a letter to the President and members of Standing Committee, ASTI, he wrote:

> It is equally obvious that the plan by Government of 're-structuring' is spurious the proposed changes in working conditions are so trivial as to attract public ridicule.

> The real reason for depriving pensioners of the benefits of the present salary increases is that the Department of Finance is concerned about the funding of future pensions. Every stratagem will be used to block the indexing of the pensions to all public servants. If the treatment of pensioners in the present package is accepted it will set a precedent and a principle for future salary negotiations. A few minor changes in working conditions will again constitute 're-structuring' and the pensioners will again be short-changed.[79]

Michael Turner and the other Dublin based members of the RSTA action group were closely associated with a recently formed group called the Public Service Pensions Action Group (PSPAG). This group was particularly active in lobbying politicians, writing to newspapers and picketing Dáil Éireann in support of their claim for the retention of pension parity. They lacked negotiating rights with the Government and were dependent on the goodwill of their former unions to support their case. Meanwhile the public sector trade unions acting through the Public Services Committee of the Irish Congress of Trade Unions would appear to have been more concerned with the wages and conditions of their active members than their retired members. In the circumstances it was inevitable that a high level of tension would emerge between trade union officials and the representatives of their retired members. This tension was not confined to any one group in the public sector. The negotiations on the PCW had been ongoing since 1994 and the element of productivity had been causing trouble in many unions.

A letter from Charlie Lennon, General Secretary of the ASTI was read at a meeting of the RSTA committee on March 13th 1997 in which he stated that a letter which had been sent by the RSTA was to be raised at the next meeting of the ASTI Standing Committee. It was also noted at that meeting that no firm decision had yet been made about the pensions of retired secondary teachers and that the matter was still under discussion by the various public bodies and that it seemed likely that a common denominator would be found. There was also some discussion at that meeting about the feasibility of a creation of the proposed RSTA Branch. It was noted that there was no provision in the RSTA constitution for the winding up of the association. If the motion to establish an ASTI branch was passed at the ASTI Annual Convention then an invitation would be sent to Pat King, Senior Official, ASTI to speak on the new branch and the services which would be available to members of the RSTA. It was quite clear that two major topics concerning the RSTA were the pension parity issue and the proposal for an RSTA branch within the ASTI. Pat King had devoted considerable time and energy to the latter issue, which was due to come before the ASTI Annual Convention at Easter but fault lines were beginning to emerge between the ASTI and the RSTA on the pension parity. It was also becoming clear that there were tensions developing within the RSTA between those members who were happy with the ASTI response to the PCW and those who were unhappy.

The Annual General meeting of the RSTA was held in the Great Southern Hotel, Galway, on Thursday April 17th 1997. It had been organised by the western section of the RSTA, which included Margaret Stewart, Kevin Kilgarriff and Tadhg McCrohan. There was a considerable attendance of members from Dublin, Kerry, Cork, Carlow and Galway. It was noted that the motion on the proposals to form an RSTA branch had not been debated at the ASTI Annual Convention, which also had taken place in Galway on Easter week but that it would be proposed at a Special Rules Convention on May 17th. It was noted that the ASTI had appointed Mary McDonnell to act as a liaison officer with the RSTA and this was much appreciated. Two important motions were passed at the AGM. The first concerned the procedures to be adopted in the event that the RSTA were to be dissolved. It was agreed that it would require a resolution passed by at least three fourths of the members of the association present and voting at a special meeting. This was a clear indication that the delegates were not entirely happy with the proposal to establish an RSTA branch despite the goodwill that had been engendered by the appointment of the liaison officer. In the event the branch proposals were defeated at the ASTI Special Convention in May.

The second motion, which was proposed by Michael Turner, was to put further pressure on the ASTI. It read "That the ASTI be asked to give moral and sufficient financial support to enable a retired secondary teacher to take a test case in the courts in order to maintain the parity of pensions for secondary teachers."[80] The motion was passed by a majority vote.

What harmony and unity of purpose appeared to have existed at the AGM in April 1997 seemed to disappear over the following months. Reporting to an RSTA committee meeting in June, Seán Geraghty, who had attended the ASTI Rules Convention in May, reported not only that the proposal to establish the RSTA as a branch had been defeated but also that he had detected a note of dissatisfaction with ASTI leadership among some of the delegates to the convention.[81] In response Margaret Stewart said that she wanted it put on the record that relations between the ASTI and the RSTA were good.[82] Michael Turner agreed that good relations should be maintained but that they should endeavour to increase membership, which at the time stood at 128. Turner also reported on a meeting of the Public Service Pensions Action Group, which had been held in the Mansion House in May. He reported that those who spoke at that meeting had expressed the opinion that unions were not concerned with pensioners and they stressed that they would have to fight their own cause. He said that each political parity had been informed of their views but as a General Election was due to take place on the following Friday no party was prepared to give a definite commitment on the question of pension parity. In the month prior to the election Peter Kerr, Seán Geraghty, Máirín O'Flynn and Michael Turner had sent numerous letters to Government Ministers, newspapers and periodicals drawing attention to the parity issue.[83] In the General Election of June 6th 1997 the Rainbow Coalition of Fine Gael, Labour and Democratic Left was defeated and was replaced by a coalition of Fianna Fáil and the Progressive Democrats. The change in Government did not foreshadow an improvement in the pension parity issue.

The next committee meeting of the RSTA, held on June 10th 1997 would appear to have been a particularly testy affair. Michael Turner was questioned as to his relationship with PSPAG and in reply he stated that work being undertaken by him and other members regarding public servants' pensions was undertaken in a private capacity and in conjunction with various pension groups. He said that any information disclosed to the RSTA would have to be at the discretion of those members.

It was reported to the meeting that the RSTA had been represented at the AGM of the National Federation of Pensioners' Associations (NFPA), on June 17th by Peter Kerr and Michael Turner. The AGM had accepted resolutions from the RSTA on home carers, taxation, pensioners' savings and the recognition of pensioners as social partners in negotiations that affect the interests of pensioners. The RSTA Vice President, Margaret Stewart, asked why the resolutions had not been discussed by the committee. She felt that it was a serious breach of procedure that delegates should find themselves defending resolutions, which had been submitted to the NFPA without previously being discussed by the committee.

In reply, the then Secretary, Máirín O'Flynn said that resolutions had been sought at the Dublin coffee morning on May 7th and they had to be submitted to the NFPA before May 30th but as there had been no committee meetings between these dates she had submitted the resolutions in good faith. Margaret Stewart queried why the resolution had not been brought to the attention of the committee at the meeting on June 3rd. Máirín O'Flynn acknowledged her error on this account and it was decided that in the future members would be asked to submit resolutions during the year so that the committee could give due consideration to them before they were finally submitted to the NFPA.

It was clear that tensions were rising between various elements on the committee. The western section had done considerable work in promoting the RSTA in the Galway region, yet many decisions appeared to be made by members in the Dublin section. Even then, not all Dublin based members of the committee were in agreement and the Treasurer, Éilís Delaney had also run up against some opposition when she sought to have a circular sent to all members concerning a trip to Howth Golf Club. Margaret Stewart had a similar experience when she sought to organise a trip to Coole Park with poetry readings and a lunch at Ballyvaughan. Earlier in the meeting of June 30th the President, Peter Kerr, had ruled that letters should only be sent to members in the western region concerning the visit to Coole and members in the greater Dublin region about the visit to Howth.[84]

Towards the end of the meeting it was reported that a letter was being sent to Micheál Martin, the newly appointed Minister for Education and that Fianna Fáil Deputies Seán Haughey and Ivor Callelly had been lobbied on the pension parity issue. Peter Kerr asked if there had been any response from the western politicians and if they had been approached. Margaret Stewart said that she was unaware of any contact being made directly with politicians but that during work in the election campaign she noted that pensions were a major issue on the doorstep. Peter Kerr urged her to contact Bobby Molloy and other local representatives. As the meeting was about to conclude Kevin Kilgarriff asked that a minute's silence be observed as a mark of respect to the late Máire MacDonagh, former General Secretary of the ASTI and Honorary Member of the RSTA. The minute's silence was observed and the meeting concluded.

After the meeting ended Peter Kerr announced his intention to resign as President and nominated the Vice President, Margaret Stewart, to act as President in his place. The Honorary Secretary, Máirín O'Flynn also indicated her intention to resign. They were informed by other committee members that as the meeting had concluded their resignations could not be accepted and they were urged to remain in office so as to restore confidence and to clarify the differences which had become apparent at recent meetings. It was agreed that a special meeting should be convened to try to resolve outstanding differences. The first item on the agenda for that meeting was a motion that the committee had full confidence in the officers elected at the last AGM. The second and third items were concerned with due process and the conduct of the meeting. The meeting was held in ASTI House on August 12th 1997 where it was agreed that a further meeting to resolve the outstanding issues would be held in the Royal Dublin Hotel on September 11th 1997. The decision to hold the meeting in the Royal Dublin Hotel rather than the ASTI Head Office was a fear among some members of the committee that their deliberations in ASTI House might be overheard. It is fair to say that a very high degree of distrust had been building up between some members of the RSTA and the ASTI over the two major issues of the proposed ASTI branch and the non-resolution of the pension parity issue.

A week after the acrimonious June meeting Máirín O'Flynn formally submitted her resignation as Secretary to the then President and sent copies of her resignation to all committee members.[85] Nonetheless she sent out a notice and an agenda for the meeting scheduled for August 12th. Margaret Stewart suggested that the meeting should be held in conjunction with the coffee morning in Wynn's Hotel on August 6th and that consideration could be given to other matters such as the Annual Dinner and the two outings proposed for September.[86] In the event the letter of notification had already issued and the agreed agenda could not be altered. The meeting of August 12th ended in disorder. Three members resigned and four members including the Secretary walked out in disgust at the acrimony of the meeting.

The next committee meeting, held on September 11th 1997 was most unusual. Both the President, Peter Kerr and the Vice President Margaret Stewart had resigned as had the Honorary Secretary, Máirín O'Flynn and in addition, Kevin Kilgarriff had submitted an oral resignation. Michael Turner, who despite a recurring health problem had worked to heal the rift, assumed the chair and Seán Geraghty acted as secretary. As Peter Kerr's resignation had never been considered by the committee his letter of resignation was withdrawn and he was reinstated as President. In addition to the resignations the Honorary Treasurer Éilís Delaney had not been attending meetings and attempts to contact her had proved fruitless. It was clear that the committee of the RSTA was seriously divided between those who favoured a social element and those who sought to pursue the pension parity issue. The former group seemed more inclined to identify with Charlie Lennon, General Secretary of the ASTI with the latter group keen to emphasise their independence. These matters were raised by Michael Turner in a letter to Seán Geraghty when he posed the question, "Should the RSTA concentrate on social outings or on our pensions? Is the RSTA to be an independent association or under the control of the ASTI Head Office?" [87] Despite the confused and acrimonious nature of the meetings, arrangements continued to be put in train for the Annual Dinner and the Mass for deceased members.

During September, Charlie Lennon, General Secretary of the ASTI wrote three letters to the RSTA concerning the internal operations of the association. The final letter was written to Seán Geraghty in which Lennon stated that recent developments in the RSTA had been raised at a meeting of the Standing Committee and that members of the Standing Committee had been concerned by accounts of internal difficulties in the RSTA. He wrote: "Standing Committee has decided that the ASTI should suspend its relations with the RSTA until such time as the RSTA members generally have an opportunity to regularise the situation at a properly convened and constituted general meeting."[88] This letter marked the lowest point in the relationship between the ASTI and the RSTA in the thirty-five years since the association was founded. Two further meetings of the remaining members of the RSTA committee were held on 6th and 10th October, which were largely concerned about internal affairs and the intrusion of the ASTI into these matters. Nonetheless, it was agreed to convene an Extraordinary General Meeting for October 23rd to try and resolve all outstanding matters.

The meeting was held in the Teachers' Club, Parnell Square, Dublin and was chaired by a former ASTI President Macartan MacCormack. Fewer members attended than had been at the Annual General Meeting in April. The most notable absentees were Margaret Stewart and members of the western section and the Treasurer Éilís Delaney. In the event only one side of the argument was heard but the meeting did start a healing process. Two motions were passed. The first was "That the unhappy events raised at the EGM be put behind the RSTA and that the main objectives of the RSTA be concentrated on." The second was "That all business of the RSTA conducted at all its meetings be treated with total privilege and confidentiality and that no member of the RSTA should approach the ASTI on any RSTA matter without the consent of the President and the committee of the RSTA."[89]

While the extraordinary general meeting brought peace to the internal workings of the RSTA the failure to obtain pension parity remained unresolved. In a letter to Seán Geraghty, Michael Turner said that in his opinion serious damage had been done to the RSTA by the letters sent to the members by Charlie Lennon, Éilís Delaney and Margaret Stewart and that bridges needed to be built within the association.[90] He said that he had learned that some members of the ASTI Standing Committee had been critical of the tone of the letters which had been sent from ASTI Head Office but unfortunately there did not appear to have been a proposal to deal with a request for the withdrawal of some of the allegations made in letters from Charlie Lennon. He believed that the PCW package did not need to be re-negotiated in order to preserve parity and in his opinion the breaking of parity seemed to have been agreed under some kind of separate and silent arrangement.[91]

The three principal RSTA activists in the parity campaign, Peter Kerr, Seán Geraghty and Michael Turner continued their association with the Public Service Pensions Action Group and also received support from some members of the ASTI Standing Committee such as Bernadine O'Sullivan, Helen Breathnach and Máire Ní Laoire. Despite their efforts and the well-documented case presented by Michael Turner little progress was achieved. In February 1998 Charlie Lennon wrote to Seán Geraghty stating that there were inaccuracies in the RSTA notes which had been submitted for inclusion in the next edition of ASTIR and that he would not publish the relevant paragraph. He went on to explain the difference between the long service allowance of £1000 and other allowances such as qualification or post allowances and said it was more akin to Island or Gaeltacht allowances and that the pensions of retired teachers did not benefit from the application of new allowances or allowances which they had not held while in service.[92]

The Lennon letter confirmed what some RSTA members had feared but they continued to fight for the righting of an injustice. The PCW package had been accepted by ASTI members in early 1997 and in one sense the attempt to achieve retrospective recognition for parity was a case of bolting the stable door when the horse had already bolted.

At the 1998 AGM of the RSTA, held in Wynn's Hotel, Dublin, the acting Honorary Secretary Seán Geraghty referred to the calm and workmanlike atmosphere which had prevailed in the committee since the EGM. He said that all disputes and rancour had been left behind and that even though the previous year had been a time of trial that the RSTA had come through smiling and eager to fulfil its role for the welfare of retired teachers. Peter Kerr, speaking as President of the RSTA, said that the EGM of October 1997 had established the RSTA on a firm footing as an autonomous body and had regularised the situation with the ASTI, with which they hoped to have continued good relations. Peter Kerr retired as president and was replaced by Seán Geraghty. Most members of the outgoing national committee did not seek re-election and were replaced by new members who had not been involved in the upsets of the previous year. Michael Turner did not seek re-election but together with Peter Kerr and Seán Geraghty, continued to seek the payment of the £1000 long service increment for teachers who had retired before the PCW was accepted. They did this in a private capacity.

Michael Turner predicted the establishment of a pensions commission. "He remained a staunch champion of the cause of public service pensioners and his acumen and leadership in this area was widely acknowledged not only by retired teachers but also by the affiliated members of the Retired Public Service Employees Association (formerly the Public Service Pensions Action Group).[93] Michael Turner exhibited many of the same characteristics that had been displayed by George Lodge more than thirty years earlier. Both were highly intelligent men, gifted with an extraordinary sense of commitment. The documents prepared by Michael Turner in 1997 and 1998 to support the case for pension parity are remarkable in the range and depth of their analysis. They are even more remarkable when it is realised that they were the product of one man unassisted with back up or secretarial services. The humanity of the man is probably best displayed in an article he wrote entitled "The End of Pension Parity?" where his thought processes closely resemble those of George Lodge.

> If the worker and later the pensioner is a person, a conscious and free subject, capable of acting in a planned and rational manner, capable of deciding about himself, with a tendency to self-realisation, do these considerations not imply a right to an income which allows workers to live a truly human life and to fulfil their family obligations in a worthy manner? The determination of a basic minimum income and a related pension is the most essential issue in the whole area of pensions. Unless basic incomes and pensions are adequate, social dynamite is more certain than a demographic time bomb."[94]

Michael Turner continued to attend RSTA meetings even as his health failed. Speaking at the 1999 AGM of the RSTA he said that all members of the association should be notified about all social outings so as to promote solidarity and friendship among members.[95] Michael Turner died on January 24th 2000, in his 77th year and at the next meeting of the RSTA committee on February 9th 2000 it was proposed to send flowers to his widow on February 24th, that being the months mind of his death.

CHAPTER 7:
RENEWAL AND EXPANSION
OF THE RSTA, 1997-2003

From its inception in 1962 the RSTA had been largely Dublin based. While there had been some members from outside the capital most social activities were centred in Dublin or were based on trips from Dublin. In order to counterbalance the over-dependence on Dublin it was decided in the early eighties that alternate AGMs would be held outside Dublin.

The first such meeting was held in the Great Southern Hotel, Galway, in 1984 and subsequently further meetings were held in Limerick, Athlone, Kilkenny and Thurles. At the 1996 AGM, which was held in the Royal Dublin Hotel on 2nd May there were delegates from Kerry, Galway, Cork, Kilkenny, Wicklow and Dublin. Margaret Stewart from Galway was elected to the National Committee and was subsequently nominated to be part of a four-person delegation to negotiate with the ASTI in relation to issues involving the PCW. There would appear to have been a renewed dynamism within the RSTA at that time with a very active participation by Galway members, which in addition to Margaret Steward included Tadhg McCrohan and Kevin Kilgarriff. They were particularly concerned with recruitment of members from outside the Dublin area and were anxious that communications should be improved, possibly through the issuing of a regular newsheet.[96] The recently elected treasurer, Éilís Delaney proposed that newly retired secondary teachers should be given six months free membership as an inducement to join the RSTA.

At the next meeting of the National Committee held on 11th September 1996, Margaret Stewart reported that she hoped to start a branch of the RSTA in Galway. She said that she felt that she could count on at least twelve members joining the new branch. She was congratulated by the other committee members on her efforts and it was proposed that a starting fund of £100 be allotted for the venture. The Galway group was particularly active in trying to establish the new branch and at a committee meeting on 18th November 1996 Margaret Stewart reported that the inaugural meeting would most likely take place in Rabbitte's public house in Forster Street, off Eyre Square in January. She said that she would like members of the National Committee to attend. In the event the first meeting of the Galway Branch was held in Rabbitte's pub on 27th February. It was also decided that the AGM would be held in the Great Southern Hotel on 17th April and that Margaret Stewart would make all arrangements with the hotel.

It will be recalled that the period between 1996 and 1997 was a particularly strained time in the relations between the ASTI and the RSTA. There was much discontent in the RSTA, about the perceived handling of the pension element in the PCW negotiations by the ASTI. There was also considerable anxiety about the possible effects of the creation of a single ASTI branch for the RSTA, with a role of less importance than other ASTI branches. A new set of Standing Orders was adopted for the AGM, where it was reported that the proposals to form a single RSTA branch for all members had not been discussed at the ASTI Annual Convention, which had also been held in Galway. It is interesting to note that the branch formed by Margaret Stewart and her Galway colleagues is referred to as the Galway Section in the minutes of the AGM and not as the Galway Branch. It would seem that there was a certain reluctance to use the term "branch" while the attitude of the ASTI to the formation of a single branch as proposed by Pat King was still undecided. In many ways Margaret Stewart was the person of the moment at the AGM in Galway. In less than a year she had organised the first branch outside Dublin, successfully organised the AGM in Galway and represented the RSTA at the ASTI Annual Convention. She further proposed to organise an outing to Coole Park with poetry readings and lunch at Ballyvaughan on 10th September 1997.[97]

The next meeting of the National Committee took place in the ASTI Head Office on 30th June 1997. It would seem that this meeting was a particularly acrimonious one where differences of opinion emerged between the President, Peter Kerr and the Vice-President, Margaret Stewart. While the minutes of the meeting indicate differences of opinion in relation to expenses, which were relatively trivial, the real reason for the discord may have been more associated with the attitude of the RSTA committee members to their relationship with the ASTI. It would seem that the members of the Western Section were more inclined to side with the ASTI Head office in the matter of the PCW negotiations and were unhappy with the more militant attitude displayed by the Dublin based members of the committee. Margaret Stewart was concerned that motions proposed at the recent AGM of the National Federation of Pensioners' Associations by the RSTA delegates had not been agreed by the committee. She asked "that her disappointment at the manner in which committee meetings were being handled be put on the record."[98] The President, Peter Kerr asked some direct questions about the level of lobbying of politicians that had been carried out by members of the Western Section.

After the meeting concluded the President, Peter Kerr announced his intention to resign and nominated the Vice-President as acting President in his place but as the meeting was over the matter of his resignation and that of the Honorary Secretary were put on hold. In order to restore confidence and clarify the differences, which had become apparent at recent meetings it was decided that a special meeting should be convened for 12th August 1997 at ASTI Head Office.[99] While there is no direct record of what happened at this meeting, it failed to resolve the divisions which had developed in the RSTA. The meeting ended in disorder with three members resigning while four others including the Honorary Secretary walked out in disgust at the acrimony of the meeting.[100] This was probably the lowest point in the history of the RSTA. No further meetings of the RSTA were held in the ASTI Head Office until November 2000.

The next meeting of the RSTA was held in the Royal Dublin Hotel on 11th September 1997. It was summoned under Rule 4(d) of the Association Rules in an attempt to revive the organisation. Michael Turner chaired the first part of the meeting until it was agreed that Peter Kerr's letter of resignation should be withdrawn and that he, Peter Kerr, would resume the role of President. Margaret Stewart had written a letter of resignation, which was accepted. Her work in establishing the Western Section was appreciated and it was proposed to thank her and hope was expressed that she would play a larger role in the future. The internal difficulties in the RSTA continued into the autumn of 1997 with a number of acrimonious meetings being held. There was also a problem of communication with the Treasurer, Éilís Delaney. In the words of Michael Turner the "situation of the RSTA was pathetic. Parity was the issue which should gain our attention."[101]

It was not surprising that the internal difficulties of the RSTA would reach the ears of Charlie Lennon, General Secretary of the ASTI. The Standing Committee of the ASTI considered reports of recent developments in the RSTA at its meeting of 26th September 1997. It decided that the ASTI should suspend its relations with the RSTA until such time as the RSTA members generally had an opportunity to regularise the situation at a properly convened and constituted general meeting.[102] The RSTA executive decided at a meeting on 6th October that an extraordinary general meeting should be called to deal with the non-cooperation of the treasurer and the interference by the ASTI in the affairs of the RSTA. It was decided to approach a number of retired ASTI members to see if they would be prepared to act as facilitators for the meeting. In the circumstances it was not surprising that some declined to get involved. In the event, the EGM was chaired by Macartan MacCormack, a former President of the ASTI, and was held in The Teachers Club, Parnell Square, Dublin on 23rd October 1997. On 14th October Charlie Lennon circularised all known RSTA members informing them of what he and the Standing Committee perceived were the reasons for the suspension of relations between the two organisations. He said that while he recognised the RSTA as a sovereign body and that most members were former ASTI members, in that context the ASTI would always be concerned to maintain and promote the RSTA.[103] The meeting afforded the delegates an opportunity to express their pent up anger with what had been happening. Don Kelly was particularly critical of the ASTI saying "the ASTI have [sic] failed abysmally and shamefully to protect the RSTA."[104] He condemned the gross interference of the ASTI in the affairs of the RSTA and he said that the ASTI wanted to put the RSTA into one branch, wouldn't publish reports of the RSTA in ASTIR and had refused emeritus membership to certain members of the RSTA.[105] Two motions were adopted unanimously at the meeting:

Motion 1: That the unhappy events raised at the EGM be put behind the RSTA and that the main objectives of the RSTA be concentrated on.

Motion 2: That all business of the RSTA conducted at all its meetings be treated with total privilege and confidentiality and that no member of RSTA should approach the ASTI on any RSTA matter without the consent of the President and Committee of he RSTA.

Following the adoption of the motions by the meeting, Peter Kerr was reaffirmed as President. Don Kelly was elected Acting Vice-President, Carmel Kelly Acting Treasurer and Seán Geraghty Acting Secretary pending confirmation at the Annual General Meeting.

In many ways the old guard had been reaffirmed in the RSTA. However, tension still remained between the RSTA and Charlie Lennon over the handling of the pension parity issue in the PCW and the manner in which only one side of the argument had been presented at the Standing Committee meeting of 26th December.

Michael Turner reflected on these matters in a letter to Don Kelly.[106] He said that the troubles in the RSTA over the previous six months led him to look at the Rules. He said that if the Rules had been followed that some of the troubles could have been avoided. Nevertheless, he believed that "the Rules needed revising especially regarding membership, branches, the functions of officers and financial arrangements."[107] He expressed the view that he was reasonably happy with the EGM and was particularly pleased with the way it had been handled by Macartan MacCormack. He said he was disappointed with the attendance but understood that some members would not wish to attend where acrimony was to be expected. He noted that there had been significant absentees: all western members and those who complained to the ASTI Head Office. He believed that significant damage had been done to the RSTA by the letters sent to the members by Charlie Lennon, Éilís Delaney and Margaret Stewart. He felt that "that bridges would need to be built possibly through an appropriate newsletter, the efforts of a National Organiser and the end of interference from the ASTI Head Office."[108]

It had been a particularly traumatic time in the history of the RSTA. There can be no doubt but that there was a significant personality clash among the members of the officer board. There had been certain failures in communication and these were not readily acknowledged. The failure of the PCW to extend parity to retired teachers was a cause of great concern not only to members of the RSTA but also to many serving teachers who were not at all happy with the PCW. Many members of the ASTI were unhappy that degree allowances were to be awarded to 9,000 primary teachers, who had followed a two-year training course. They perceived continued erosion in their salary structure, which had begun with the Common Basic Salary proposed in the Ryan Report of 1968.[109]

The Extraordinary General Meeting on 23rd October 1997 brought closure to what had been a particularly acrimonious six months in the RSTA. Margaret Stewart was true to her word. In her letter of resignation from the National Committee she wished the RSTA and its Committee success in the important work of serving the interests of retired teachers and indicated that she would continue to work as Honorary Secretary of the Western Section of the RSTA.[110] She was the organiser of the Western Section, which was effectively the first branch of the RSTA to be established outside Dublin, and has remained a stalwart of that branch up to the present time.

At the next meeting of the RSTA Committee after the EGM Michael Turner proposed that a National Organiser be appointed to try to boost numbers.[111] Don Kelly had already proposed that an attempt should be made to try to recruit retired teachers who were members of religious orders. The ASTI specifically barred the recruitment of members of religious orders because of their perceived close association with management. But times were changing and since the late 1980s when Boards of Management had been established in voluntary secondary schools a number of lay principals had been appointed, some of whom had been prominent ASTI members. It is interesting to note that Michael Turner was one of the first laymen to have been appointed Principal of a Catholic voluntary secondary school in Ireland when he was appointed to that post in Templeogue College, Dublin, in 1977. He was succeeded in that position in 1987 by Ray Kennedy, who had been President of the ASTI in 1983-84. Despite Don Kelly's contacts with the Council of Managers of Catholic Secondary Schools (CMCSS) there was very little recruitment from that quarter.

No decision was made on the appointment of a National Organiser but at a subsequent meeting on 14th January 1998 a discussion took place on the possibility of circularising all ASTI Branch Secretaries and Principals of secondary schools to inform them of the existence of the RSTA and to elicit their support in contacting retired teachers. No decision was taken on that proposal and the one definite proposal to emerge came from Michael Turner who said "If each member recruited one new member it would be a start."[112] It was also agreed to recruit retired Community and Comprehensive School Principals into the RSTA. This allowed for the recruitment of Pádraig Heeran, a former ASTI Vice-President and retired Principal of Tallaght Community School, who was to play an important role in the still unresolved parity issue

At the RSTA committee meeting on 29th September 1998 Peter Kerr proposed and Sarah Scott (Treasurer) seconded that £100 should be sent to the Western Section to cover administration costs and that a further £50 should be enclosed for social purposes.[113] It would seem that despite the differences, which had arisen, between Kerr and Margaret Stewart in the previous year, the work of Stewart in Galway was much appreciated.

The election of Sarah Scott as treasurer at the AGM in 1998 was a significant development. Not only did she re-organise the financial affairs but she was very concerned with membership records and organisation. While Michael Turner had, at an earlier stage, proposed the creation of a position of national organiser, this had not happened. This role was undertaken by Scott. In January 1999 membership cards and a newsletter were sent to all members. In the same month the new President, Seán Geraghty indicated his intention to re-establish good relations with the ASTI and to renew the coffee mornings in the ASTI Head Office. He reported that he had met with members of the Western Section and that he would like to extend the link to Cork and Limerick.[114] At the same meeting Peter Kerr proposed that a letter should be sent to the Steering Committee of the ASTI Annual Convention seeking permission for the RSTA President to address the convention.[115]

A delegation comprising Seán Geraghty, Peter Kerr, Sarah Scott and Máirín O'Flynn travelled to Cork on 29th April 1999 for the purposes of establishing a regional section of the RSTA. At the RSTA AGM the following week the President, Seán Geraghty was able to report that a branch had been established in Cork and in the subsequent elections Humphrey Twomey from Cork was elected Vice-President, thus consolidating the link with Cork.[116] Geraghty also acknowledged the thriving Galway Branch and said that he was looking forward to travelling to Limerick, Waterford, Wexford and Athlone to extend the Branch structure. He was also most grateful for the assistance of the elected members of the ASTI who had helped in the restoration of good relations with that union. He particularly singled out the help given by Michael Corley, President, Bernadine O'Sullivan, Vice-President and Helen Breathnach, Honorary National Organiser.[117]

The spirit of goodwill and reconciliation was set to continue. A meeting between the two bodies took place in the ASTI Head Office on 25th August 1999. The ASTI was represented by Bernadine O'Sullivan (then ASTI President), Charlie Lennon, Helen Breathnach and Michael Ward (ASTI Treasurer). The RSTA delegation comprised Seán Geraghty, Sarah Scott and Eileen Brennan. The ASTI offered to purchase a computer for the use of the RSTA and to provide training in its use. It was also agreed that the ASTI subvention would continue and that members would continue to receive copies of ASTIR.[118] It would appear that the rift, which had begun to emerge two and a half years earlier, had been healed but that the parity issue still remained unresolved. Later that year it was decided that three newsletters should be sent to the members each year and that a sub-committee was to be established to decide on the articles to be printed. The general air of goodwill persisted and it was decided to invite Bernadine O'Sullivan, Helen Breathnach, Charlie Lennon and Michael Ward as guests to the Christmas Lunch in Cassidy's Hotel, Cavendish Row, Dublin.[119] The ASTI continued to give support to the RSTA, not only by way of subvention but also by the work of Joanne McGuire in the Head Office and it was decided to give her a gift voucher for £25 as a Christmas gift.[120]

The new millennium dawned brightly for the RSTA. At the February 2000 meeting of the Committee Tony Burke of the recently established Cork Branch reported on a recent meeting with the Minister for Education, Mícheál Martin. While no improvement had been made on the parity issue at least an audience had been given. James McSweeney proposed that further branches of the RSTA should be established in Kilkenny and Limerick and it was noted that Gerry Costigan, business manager of ASTIR had offered free advertising space to the RSTA for the purpose of recruiting new members. Seán Geraghty agreed to contact the Department of Education in Athlone to try to get names and addresses of recently retired secondary teachers. The only dark cloud was due to the untimely death of Michael Turner who died in January.[121]

With the introduction of the Euro it was decided that the annual subscription would be €18 and not £15 and of that, €7 would be returned to each branch. The Honorary Secretary, Nuala O'Connor reported to the 2002 AGM that in the previous year new branches had been established in Wicklow, Wexford, Kerry and Sligo and that contact had been made between the Wicklow and Kilkenny branches.[122] She also mentioned that a letter had been received from the Retired Branch of the NASUWT in Belfast suggesting that some form of liaison or exchange of ideas might be mutually beneficial. The then Treasurer, Tony Burke, reported that there was a closing balance of €12,000 in the account but that the Treasurer's task was becoming more onerous as the numbers increased and it would be a great help if a system of "deduction at source" could be introduced for annual subscriptions.[123]

By 2002 the RSTA was more united and confident in itself than it had been five years earlier. Cordial relations had been restored with the ASTI. The finances were on a much sounder footing, mainly through the offices of Sarah Scott, Tony Burke and Tomás McCathmhaoil. As an association it had finally broken out of the confines of the Dublin area and had succeeded in establishing a number of provincial branches. The spirit that was evident at the AGM on 8th May 2002 was in stark contrast to that which had obtained at the extraordinary general meeting on 23rd October 1997, when there was a strong likelihood that the RSTA would implode and self-destruct. When Humphrey Twomey succeeded Sarah Scott as President in 2002 there was no reference to the fact that it was the 40th anniversary of the association but it was clear that the RSTA had been firmly established and was set to continue in an expansionary mode.

CHAPTER 8:
THE RE-ESTABLISHMENT OF THE PENSIONS SUB-COMMITTEE, ASTI

The Pensions Sub-Committee, ASTI was established as a result of the convening of a Special Convention on pensions by the ASTI, which was held in the Burlington Hotel, Dublin on 2nd October 2004. There had been a growing concern among ASTI members about what they perceived as the diminution in their pension entitlements since the mid-nineties.

This diminution was first noticed when the terms of the PCW as applied to teachers created a break in parity between retired teachers and those who were still working. This was further exacerbated by the stipulation that all new entrants to the public service would be required to pay a full contribution to PRSI from 5th April 1995. The requisition notice under which the Special Convention had been called had been signed by more than the required 800 signatories. Its desired purpose was "(a) to debate the unilateral changes being imposed on pensions of new, serving and retired teachers and other public service employees and (b) to consider an appropriate response."[124]

Bernadine O'Sullivan, who had largely been responsible for collecting the requisite 800 signatures, alluded to the fact that it was the tenth anniversary of the convening of the last ASTI convention on pensions. In a long opening address she forensically examined the more recent developments in regard to pensions. She acknowledged that there had been some improvements made as a result of the PCW, which facilitated teachers to retire at 55 years and to receive a pro-rata pension. She commended the ASTI for its efforts in that regard but she went on to say that the Public Service Superannuation Act, 2004 had changed matters. She said that the act had put into effect some of the recommendations of the Commission on Public Service Pensions, which had been set up by the Government in the late 90s. As a result teachers, in the future, would not be able to access their pensions until they were 65. This was a worse situation than that which had existed up until the PCW - at least until then one could retire at 60 on a pro-rata basis without a penalty clause. She concluded her speech by saying that she was not in the business of scaremongering and was merely presenting information. She said that she believed that the best thing that could be done was "to set up a committee to monitor these things rather than having our negotiators ambushed.[125]

The next speaker was Pádraig Heeran, a former Vice-President of the ASTI and a retired Community School Principal. Heeran had been actively involved in the Retired Public Service Association in the late nineties and he told Convention of his experiences at that time. He said that it was his opinion that it did not matter what Government was in power but that public service pensions would be targeted in the future. He instanced the disparity in pension payments enjoyed by former government Ministers and retired public servants and made special reference to the pension and gratuity enjoyed by former Minister for Education, Mary O'Rourke.[126] Eight further delegates spoke to the convention and finally a number of motions were proposed and adopted. The principal one was:

> That this Special Convention elect a sub-committee, which will monitor the impact of changes to the pensions of teachers. Said sub-committee will report to Annual Convention 2005 with recommendations as to the appropriate responses to any change, which will adversely affect the pensions of teachers, and will be re-elected biannually as and from Annual Convention 2006.

It was agreed that the sub-committee should be composed of five members and that Bernadine O'Sullivan should act as convenor. Nine delegates were nominated to contest the election for the other four places, which resulted in the election of Louis O'Flaherty, Michael Freeley, Joe Moran and Niamh Walker. O'Flaherty was a member of the RSTA but the others were still serving teachers. The first meeting of the sub-committee took place on 22nd November 2004 and the first decision made was that the operating principle of the committee should be the protection of the Secondary Teachers' Superannuation Scheme from any attempts to diminish its value to members. It was the unanimous opinion of the members that pension was deferred pay and, as such should not suffer any diminution The sub-committee also considered three further motions, which had been adopted at the Special Convention. They were about seeking the services of an actuary to assess the benefits of the existing scheme, to place advertisements in newspapers informing the public about the damage to pensions and to mount a legal challenge on equality grounds to the Government's new pension arrangements, which had come into force for newly appointed public servants since April 1st 2004. In each case the pensions sub-committee decided that these matters were more appropriate for the Standing Committee of the ASTI and not for a sub-committee.

At the next meeting of the Pensions Sub-Committee on 9th December a letter from Norma Murray, Honorary Secretary of Cork North Branch was discussed. In it she asked that the sub-committee investigate the relationship between superannuation and PRSI payments under a number of headings and also that additional information be included on retired teachers' pay slips. As in the previous matters it was felt that the sub-committee could do little in these matters except to refer them to the Standing Committee. In January 2005 when the preliminary agenda for the ASTI Annual Convention was circulated it was found that no fewer than fourteen motions were concerned with superannuation and pension rights. This was no doubt due in no small manner to the issues raised at the Special Convention in the previous October. Louis O'Flaherty, acting in his capacity as President of the RSTA, wrote to all branches of the ASTI urging them to support Motion 16. This motion urged: "That the ASTI demands that the pension rights of newly appointed teachers be restored to those which pertained for all teachers prior to the 2003 budget . . ." He concluded his letter by saying "We, the retired teachers depend on you to keep the flag flying even as we tried to do so in our time."[127]

In the early years of the Pensions Sub-Committee it was felt that all increases in salary should be on basic pay and not on allowances as there was no guarantee these allowances would attract pension entitlement in the long run. There was a general feeling that pensions should not have been factored into the calculations made by the Benchmarking Body. It was a time when increasing attention was being paid to the cost of public sector pensions. There were numerous reports and recommendations on the issue, all of which were discussed and monitored by the Pensions Sub-Committee. The cost of the purchase of notional service for the purpose of pension entitlement increased and serious doubts arose as to the continuance of the early retirement scheme, which had been introduced as part of the PCW. The committee urged that every effort should be made to retain the early retirement scheme and John White, General Secretary, ASTI "assured the members that he would be doing his level best to retain those schemes."[128] At the next meeting of the sub-committee on 6th December 2006 the Deputy General Secretary, ASTI, Diarmaid de Paor reported that the early retirement scheme had been extended for a further two years.

On 17th October 2007 the Government published a Green Paper on Pensions. The sub-committee felt that the issues raised were of such importance that a summary should be published in the ASTI Convention Handbook 2008 and that the ASTI should issue a public response. At a special meeting of the sub-committee on 19th May 2008 Diarmaid de Paor reported that discussions were taking place with other teacher unions on the issue of preparing a response from the three unions to the Green paper. After a lengthy discussion the sub-committee recommended that the ASTI delegates to any joint meeting with other teachers unions should highlight:

- The important role of the Public Service

- Contributions already made by teachers to their pensions

- The lower value of pensions to new entrants

- The discounting of pensions in the Benchmarking Report

- The folly of attempting to project to 2061

- Resistance to a "race to the bottom."[129]

These points were well made in the ASTI Response to the Green Paper on Pensions, which concluded: "The fact that many private sector employers provide no pensions to their employees is to be deeply regretted and the ASTI fully supports the call by the ICTU for the introduction of mandatory pensions in the private sector. However, the suggestion by some in the private sector that the solution to the inequality in pension provision is to reduce the value of public service pensions must be resisted to the full."[130]

While the ASTI issued a response to the Green Paper, it would seem that there was a reluctance to speak too openly about the changing circumstances on pensions. An element of tension was building up between the members of the sub-committee and the ASTI officers and officials with the latter advising caution in the very strained economic situation that was evolving in the State. The ASTI continued to issue comprehensive documents on pension entitlements to its members and in November 2008 issued a special issue of Nuacht advising members of options for enhancement of pension/retirement benefits.

In March 2009 the ASTI General Secretary, John White informed the members of the Pensions Sub-Committee on the progress being made with the ASTI's legal challenge to the summary suspension of the Early Retirement Scheme for teachers. He told the sub-committee that an ex-parte injunction had been obtained. He pointed out that what was at issue was the legitimate expectations of the teachers concerned and that any success would only apply to that year. The case involved a particular group of teachers, some of whom were working in a school which was due to close and who had hoped to avail of early retirement rather than re-deployment to another school. It was also reported at that meeting that the proposed meeting with representatives of the other teacher unions to agree a common strategy in relation to pensions had not as yet taken place. The sub-committee passed a motion rejecting the imposition of the pension levy, which had recently been imposed on all public servants. It was agreed that a leaflet on pensions should be produced for distribution at the Annual Convention of the ASTI. The Chairperson, Bernadine O'Sullivan agreed to draft the leaflet and to forward it to Head Office so it would be available for distribution with other material.[131] The preparation and distribution of this leaflet was to cause some tension between members of the sub-committee and the officers and officials of the ASTI. At the next meeting of the sub-committee the members asked that the leaflet prepared by O'Sullivan for the Annual Convention be printed in ASTIR and be ascribed to the Pensions Sub-Committee.[132] The officers and officials of the ASTI indicated that there were problems about some aspects of the material included in the leaflet and the sub-committee agreed that the document should be prepared jointly by the Deputy General Secretary, ASTI, Diarmaid de Paor and Bernadine O'Sullivan. The difficulties concerning the publication of the information leaflet persisted over four meetings of the Pensions Sub-Committee. In November the ASTI President, Joe Moran and Deputy General Secretary, Diarmaid de Paor reported that the article written by O'Sullivan on behalf of the Pensions Sub-Committee had been submitted to the ASTIR Editorial Board. The board had decided not to include the article in the November issue of ASTIR but to rework it and include it in the January issue. After a long discussion the committee agreed that a motion on the issue not be adopted, in the best interest of harmony within the union and at the request of the President.[133] It is evident from the minutes and from conversations with some of those present that feelings had run high during these months in 2009 and that the elected members of the sub-committee felt an inability to convey their views to the wider ASTI membership. Eventually an article on pensions by Bernadine O'Sullivan on behalf of the Pensions Sub-Committee was published in the January 2010 edition of ASTIR.

If the members of the sub-committee felt an inability to convey their views to the wider membership it did not inhibit them from monitoring and discussing many aspects of pension entitlement which were emerging as a result of the economic downturn, which had been increasing in the State. The matter of most concern to the members of the Pensions Sub-Committee during 2009-2010 was the continued deterioration of pension entitlement for teachers. The sub-committee was very aware of the worsening of pension entitlements for younger teachers and particularly for those who had commenced teaching since 1995. The members were concerned about the abolition of the early retirement scheme and the proposal to raise the retirement age for new entrants to 66-70. They were also concerned with the introduction of the co-ordinated pension scheme which meant that those teachers who were paying a full PRSI contribution would have the pension benefits associated with that contribution included in their eventual pension. Previously, if teachers had been fortunate enough to have paid a sufficient number of PRSI contributions they could avail of contributory pensions in addition to those which might accrue from superannuation contributions. The sub-committee was very concerned about the emergence of a two-tier pension system for teachers and particularly about the impact of this development on the future strength of the ASTI as a negotiating body for all teachers both serving and retired. The sub-committee foresaw a situation when teachers working in the same schools would have different pension entitlements based on the date on which they entered the profession. It was felt that not enough had been done to counteract the media onslaught, which suggested that all public sector workers had "gold-plated" non-contributory pensions. The extent of teachers' contributions to their pensions and the failure of the State to contribute even the statutory requirements to a pension fund were not fully recognised. The Pensions Sub-Committee considered a preliminary Report by the commission of Public Services into pension arrangements in other European countries, which showed that a variety of methods was used to calculate the amounts paid to public servants. The sub-committee expressed its opposition to any change in the method for calculating pension, either by means of the consumer price index or career average. It was felt that the Superannuation Scheme and particularly the element involving parity with serving teachers had been fought for over many years and should be defended by all means. The sub-committee was of the view that an inter-union group on pensions should be formed.[134] The sentiments expressed by the sub-committee were particularly apposite in view of the subsequent decision by the Government to introduce a much reduced salary scale for newly appointed teachers.

A meeting with representatives of the TUI and the INTO took place in late 2009 and as a result it was agreed to commission a report on future pension provision, which would be paid for by the three teachers unions. The report was prepared by Trident Consulting and became known in teacher circles as the Trident Report. It was published in November 2010 and gave a very comprehensive analysis of the possible long-term effects of the proposed changes in teacher pension entitlements. It noted that "Under the Government's new proposal, the value of member contributions will exceed the value of the benefits that they will receive. This situation may be open to legal challenge."[135] All of these matters were debated and discussed in subsequent meetings of the Pensions Sub-Committee. The suggestion in the Trident Report that the changes in pension entitlement might be open to legal challenge was noted by the sub-committee and it requested the Standing Committee of the ASTI to seek legal advice on the issue. Legal advice was obtained but it was decided not to pursue the issue at that stage.[136]

In October 2012 the Pensions Sub-Committee asked that the Standing Committee would consider organising a demonstration against the introduction of a new single public service pension scheme. It also requested that a poster on pension issues be prepared and distributed. Michael Moriarty, a member of the sub-committee, had prepared a draft article on pensions, which he hoped would be published in ASTIR. The sub-committee agreed some changes and the Deputy General

Secretary, Diarmaid de Paor agreed to check the article for accuracy of figures before submitting it to the ASTIR Editorial Board. The article was subsequently published in the RSTA Newsletter.

The New Single Pension Scheme for New Entrants to the Public Service was due to come into effect on 1st January 2013. The Pensions Sub-Committee at its meeting on 4th December 2012 made the following statement:

> The Pensions Sub-Committee, having considered the Single Public Service Pension Scheme, believes that it will be open to legal challenge. They [sic] note that this scheme does not apply to members of the Oireachtas, the Judiciary or the Comptroller and Auditor General."[137]

The sub-committee further asked that a meeting be arranged between the Standing Committee, the sub-committee and a representative of Trident Consulting as early as possible in the New Year.

By 2012 the Pensions Sub-Committee had been in existence for eight years. The members had been meeting four or five times a year to examine, discuss and make recommendations on the ever-deteriorating pension entitlements of teachers. It was charged with the task of monitoring the impact of changes to the pensions of teachers and to make recommendations as to the appropriate responses to any change, which would adversely affect the pensions of teachers. The sub-committee had been true to its brief but one cannot but feel that in many ways the members had been talking to themselves.

It would appear that the ASTI, faced with the reduction in salaries and the worsening conditions being offered to newly qualified teachers, was more inclined to concentrate on the immediate problems faced by its members. During the years since 2004 many motions in relation to superannuation, the break with parity and the abandonment of the early retirement scheme were debated, discussed andadopted unanimously at the ASTI Annual conventions. Protests were made in the relevant fora, but no direct action to counteract the changes was undertaken. In the circumstances this is understandable but it may have led to a sense of frustration among some members of the Pensions Sub-Committee.

CHAPTER 9:
CONSOLIDATION IN A
CHANGED ENVIRONMENT
2003 - 2012

Like Sarah Scott, Humphrey Twomey served only one year as President but they both made a very strong contribution to the RSTA. Scott had acted as treasurer before becoming President and in that role she put the RSTA finances on a very firm footing. She also contributed, in no small way, to the expansion of the RSTA outside the confines of Dublin.

Twomey had been one of the founding members of the Cork Branch and together with Seán Lydon and Tony Burke had contributed greatly to the formation of that branch.

Speaking at the 2003 AGM in Cassidy's Hotel, Dublin, Twomey welcomed the members and outlined the history of the RSTA in relation to the seeking of pension parity and problems arising from the more recent proposals on benchmarking.[138] He drew attention to the fact that future salary increases were to be dependent on productivity and that as pensioners were no longer working he feared that they would not benefit from increases paid to serving teachers. He said that a letter had been sent by the Cork Branch of the RSTA to the General Secretary of the ASTI, Charlie Lennon and all the members of the ASTI Standing Committee seeking help on the resolution of the outstanding problem of pension parity. The Cork Branch proposal that the RSTA should be present at salary negotiations, as least as observers, met with no response.[139] He did acknowledge that some ASTI activists had given great support to the RSTA, notably Bernadine O'Sullivan, Susie Hall, Máire Ní Laoire, Helen Breathnach, Noel Buckley and the recently deceased members, Seán Lydon and Michael Turner.

While the early years of the new millennium had been reasonably tranquil and expansionary within the RSTA the same could not have been said about the internal workings of the ASTI, which was riven with internal disputes mainly associated with national wage agreements.[140] These disputes led to the ASTI withdrawing from the Irish Congress of Trade unions. It was becoming abundantly clear that the process which had been initiated during the PCW negotiations which tied salary increases to changes in work practices was becoming the norm and that any salary increases paid in this manner would not be passed on to retired teachers.

The Central Executive Council of the ASTI decided to withdraw from the ICTU on 22nd January 2000 and to pursue a salary increase of 30% on its own.[141] This action was not prompted by solidarity with retired teachers but rather with the massive increase in the cost of living, which had been brought about with the arrival of the economic boom known as the "Celtic Tiger." Workers in the private sector could earn salaries that would compensate but teachers felt powerless in the circumstances prevailing at the time. Following the withdrawal from the ICTU, the ASTI sought, without success, to negotiate its claim for a 30% increase without the assistance of the other teacher unions, the INTO and the TUI. The ASTI strategy was to embark on a series of one-day strikes and to impose a ban on the supervision of students outside of class and on voluntary cover for absent colleagues.[142] The first one-day strike was on 14th November 2000. Secondary teachers had traditionally substituted for absent colleagues and supervised students outside of the classroom. These duties had been taken as part of the job specification but were not included in any contractual obligation except in the case of some boarding schools where extra payment was sometimes made. Now that it had been introduced as part of a bargaining strategy it wasn't going to disappear. In late November 2002 the ASTI accepted a scheme of payment for substitution and supervision as part of a settlement for the long running dispute.[143] Retired teachers were aggrieved as they had done these duties for years without compensation, nor would it now be recognised in their pensions.

Retired teachers had always supported their serving colleagues. In January 2001 the RSTA issued a statement refuting any suggestion that retired teachers would be prepared to supervise or correct the State examinations should they be boycotted by the ASTI.[144] The RSTA continued to seek pension parity while at the same time supporting serving teachers. On 19th February 2002 the National Executive of the RSTA expressed its support for teachers' industrial action and decided to recommend that no retired teacher should offer his/her services to replace striking teachers. It was further decided that letters to that effect should be sent to Charlie Lennon and to George O'Callaghan, General Secretary of the Joint Managerial Body (JMB).[145]

In the circumstances it was not surprising that some members of the RSTA were annoyed that a means had not been found to extend payment for substitution and supervision to those who had done it for many years without recompense. It was becoming increasingly clear that future salary increases would be based on changed work practices and that these increases would not transfer automatically to pensions. Humphrey Twomey, as President of the RSTA, had written to Charlie Lennon on the topic of substitution and supervision but the ASTI General Secretary, in his reply, had make it clear that nothing could be done on that issue but that he would continue to strive for parity in all possible ways. It was also clear that the concept of pension parity which had been conceded nearly thirty years earlier was being gradually eroded. Humphrey Twomey did not seek re-election at the 2003 AGM of the RSTA. His successor was Louis O'Flaherty.

O'Flaherty, a former President of the ASTI, had only been a member of the RSTA for a short time. He had not been involved in the more recent tribulations of the RSTA but within the ASTI he would have been well known to most of the participants, having been active in the ASTI for many years. The RSTA in 2003 had a membership of 540 and a bank balance of over €12,000, mainly due to the unstinting work of his predecessors and the commitment of the many voluntary office holders. It was decided that contact should be made with the Department of Education in Athlone so that subscriptions to the RSTA could be deducted at source from pensions. Not all members were happy with this proposal and there was a further complication as not all members of the RSTA were in receipt of their pensions from the Secondary Branch of the Department of Education and Science Some had been employed in the Community and comprehensive sector and others had been employed in Community Colleges under the administration of local Vocational Education authorities. Nonetheless, negotiations continued with the Retired Teachers Payment Section of the Department of Education and Science

(DES) and by October 2003 a scheme for the deduction of RSTA subscriptions from pension was agreed with that body, subject to comprehensive conditions.[146] One of the conditions was that all RSTA members wishing to participate in the scheme would have to sign a mandate form, which would be retained by the RSTA. If all the conditions were complied with then the first deduction would be made in May 2004.[147] The mandate forms were produced in the manner prescribed by the Department of Education and Science but there was considerable difficulty in ensuring their return to the RSTA. The work of ensuring the implementation of the scheme was entrusted to Nuala O'Connor, Catherine McHugh and Sarah Scott who liaised with the ASTI Credit Union to implement the new scheme.

As has already been noted, concern had been increasing among members of the RSTA that pension parity was being eroded. The first indication of this trend was with the PCW arrangements of the mid-nineties when a special allowance of £1,000 per annum, payable to all teachers who had been ten years on the maximum point of the salary scale was not recognised for pension purposes for those who had already retired. In the years since 1996 there had been a considerable number of younger retirees who had benefited from the early retirement options that had been made available through the PCW. Some of these would have received the special allowance while still working and would therefore have received it as a proportion of their final salary. There was an increasing sense of frustration among the members of the RSTA. They lacked negotiation rights and while the ASTI as parent body had renewed cordial relations with the RSTA, after the upheavals of the late nineties, the union was primarily concerned with the salaries of its working and subscribing members. Humphrey Twomey, as already noted, in his presidential address to the 2003 AGM outlined the history of efforts made by the RSTA to deal with the issues of parity and benchmarking and his frustration in trying to progress the issue with the ASTI Head Office.[148] He did, however, single out for mention some elected members of the ASTI who had been particularly helpful to him.[149]

It was one of these elected members, Bernadine O'Sullivan, who emerged as champion of the retired members. O'Sullivan had supported Michael Turner in the earlier campaign. She had been elected President of the ASTI in 1999 and had been opposed to the concept of benchmarking. She had sought election to Seanad Éireann in 2002 and had very publicly raised the issue of public sector pension in her campaign literature. In early 2004 she produced a document which outlined the deterioration of pension entitlements since 1996.[150] In it she stated "When the radical new way of paying all public servants, namely Benchmarking, is fully operational, with its emphasis on performance and productivity, the Government will be able to plead that those who have retired are not entitled to certain increases because they have not given any extra productivity."[151] In the document she calculated that teacher pensioners who had retired after 40 years service should be in receipt of nearly €2,000 more per annum than they were currently receiving. She alleged that payment for Supervision and Substitution was non-core payment and while the ASTI had succeeded in its campaign to make it pensionable for those who undertook to carry out the duties, it was not passed on to pensioners who had already done this work.

The points raised by O'Sullivan were picked up by O'Flaherty in his presidential address to the AGM of the RSTA in 2004. He decried the continuous erosion of pension parity and he urged that serving teachers should be reminded never to lose sight of pensions. He said that the influence of pensioners was limited insofar as they could not go on strike. He also said that the RSTA should talk to other pension groups but that it was exceedingly difficult to influence political decisions.[152]

In the autumn of 2004 Bernadine O'Sullivan and other concerned members of the ASTI set about gathering 800 signatures for a petition to hold a special convention on teachers' pensions. The issue of pension parity had been a contentious issue within the ASTI and the RSTA for nearly ten years and O'Sullivan had been very supportive of all attempts to retain pension parity. The requisite number of signatories was secured and the special convention was held in the Burlington Hotel, Dublin on 2nd October 2004. In her opening address to the convention O'Sullivan gave a comprehensive account as to how pension parity had suffered over recent salary agreements. She said that she was not in the business of scare-mongering, that she was merely presenting facts and that the best thing that they could do was to set up a committee to monitor developments so that they would not be ambushed in any negotiations with the Government.[153] Pádraig Heeran, a former Vice-President of ASTI and retired Principal of Tallaght Community School traced the history of pension parity and how it had been achieved in 1973. (It should be remembered that while pension parity had been granted in 1973 a time lapse had been imposed on the awarding of increases to pensioners. This was not resolved until 1983 when it was agreed that increases in pensions would occur at the same time as pay increases to serving teachers). Heeran had been active in the earlier campaign with Michael Turner, Peter Kerr and Seán Geraghty. He instanced the case where his successor as Principal was paid a considerably higher salary than he was, under the terms of re-structuring but that he, Heeran, did not receive a similar increase in his pension. He said that the group he represented had "lobbied Government Ministers, the Opposition and the Irish Congress of Trade Unions, where we got a very hostile reception."[154] Numerous speakers including RSTA President Louis O'Flaherty spoke in the debate. He said that he had been fighting issues concerning teachers in various fora for over forty years. He told delegates that they had seen a lot of turmoil in teaching unions and in the ASTI in particular in the last eight years.[155] He went on to say that it had always been a fundamental tenet of trade unionism that pension is deferred salary but when he and others drew attention to the anomalies in the PCW that they were laughed at and ridiculed. He concluded by saying that he believed that the stable door was still open and that the horse had not yet bolted and if they hurried they might be able to slam the door shut.

After considerable debate a motion to establish a sub-committee to monitor the impact of changes to the pensions of teachers was put to the convention and was carried nem con . It was agreed that the sub-committee would be composed of five members and that it would report to the ASTI Annual Convention 2005, with recommendations as to the appropriate responses to any changes, which would adversely affect the pensions of teachers. It would be elected biennially as and from Annual Convention 2006.[156] This decision meant that a permanent sub-committee on pensions had been established in the ASTI and that the initial convenor would be Bernadine O'Sullivan. In the event, O'Flaherty was also elected to the committee, thereby ensuring that the RSTA had a voice on the pensions issue within the ASTI. It did not mean that the RSTA would have any negotiating rights but it did allow for a mechanism to enable the views of the RSTA to be conveyed to an important sub-committee of the ASTI.

O'Flaherty reported on the proceedings of the Special Convention to the next meeting of the RSTA Committee and on the strategies to be adopted.[157] It was also agreed at that meeting that an extra member should be co-opted to the National Committee to help with the increased workload which had come about as a result of the increasing membership and a wider involvement with like minded organisations. It was decided that Marie Doyle, Secretary of the Dublin Branch, should be co-opted.

In the early years of the RSTA a report of its activities was included in the handbook for the ASTI Annual Convention. This practice had been discontinued in the 1980s and reports of RSTA activities were printed in ASTIR. In 2003 Humphrey Twomey was invited to address the ASTI Annual Convention. He made a strong plea for pension parity. The facility to address Annual Convention has continued since 2003 and it affords an opportunity for the RSTA President to apprise the Convention delegates of RSTA affairs.

The 2004 AGM of the RSTA was held in ASTI Head Office. This was a clear indication that the tensions, which had emerged ten years earlier between the ASTI and the RSTA, had finally been resolved. It was also noted that RSTA delegates had attended the AGMs of the retired INTO, TUI and NASUWT in the previous year and had also attended two conferences of the National Federation of Pensioners' Associations. Among the motions passed at the AGM was one deploring the fact that retired secondary teachers who had been registered under the terms of the Secondary Teachers Registration Council would no longer be registered under the terms of the newly established Teaching Council. As a result, they would not be permitted to vote in the electoral process for that body.[158] This exclusion was an annoyance but as the RSTA did not have negotiating rights and as most members did not have any particular desire to return to the classroom it remained a mere irritant.

Meanwhile, the still serving teaching body of the ASTI was becoming increasingly aware of the threat to the future pensions of its members. Some were mindful of the earlier dispute concerning the terms of the PCW. It was in that context that Motion 34 was passed at the ASTI Annual Convention in 2003. The motion read "That this convention re-iterates ASTI policy that the principle of full pension parity be restored and preserved in all future pay negotiations."[159] The motion was proposed by John O'Sullivan, of the Dublin South West Branch, who had first hand knowledge of the work undertaken by Michael Turner in the earlier campaign and was seconded by Brendan Broderick who was to become President of the ASTI in 2011. The following year an even more prescient motion, Motion 22 was carried at the ASTI Annual Convention, which stated "That all new teachers receive the same pension rights as existing teachers."[160] While the National Committee of the RSTA was aware of these developments it was limited in the degree of support which it could offer towards achieving the aims and objectives contained in what were aspirational motions.

Speaking at a National Committee meeting of the RSTA in January 2005 the President, Louis O'Flaherty reported that of the 112 motions on the preliminary agenda for the ASTI Annual Convention that 14 were concerned with pensions. He said that in his opinion the most comprehensive motion was Motion 16, which read "That the ASTI demands that the pension rights of newly appointed teachers be restored to those that pertained for all teachers prior to the 2003 Budget and seeks to join with other unions in order to take appropriate industrial action if any attempt is made to introduce a two-tier retirement scheme or to reduce the benefits currently available to serving or retired teachers under the terms of the existing superannuation scheme." O'Flaherty said that it was most important that as many ASTI branches as possible should support the motion and he proposed that the RSTA should circularise all 55 branches of the ASTI urging support for the motion.[161]

In the period 2002 - 2008 there had been considerable expansion in the RSTA. In 2000 there were only 186 paid up members while there was a notional membership of 245. Branches outside of Dublin had been established in Cork and Galway and there were further plans to establish branches in Limerick, Kilkenny and Wexford.[162] This increase in membership had been achieved mainly by the dedicated work of members of the national Executive who worked unceasingly to expand the organisation. Advertisements had been placed in ASTIR seeking new members and from 2000 the RSTA President had been invited to address ASTI Annual Conventions. In 2000 the ASTI gave a present of a computer to the RSTA and this was used to good effect to keep track of membership. RSTA notes were published in every issue of ASTIR and a series of newsletters were posted to all members. Members of the National Committee started to visit newly formed branches and encouraged them to make contact with other branches. Plans were made so that annual subscriptions could be deducted from pensions by the DES or by direct debit. This ensured a steady flow of income, which was complemented by an annual subvention from the ASTI. A recruitment leaflet was prepared and a booklet listing the entitlements of retired teachers was compiled by Eileen Brennan, Nuala O'Connor and Nuala Carroll. The latter project was sponsored by Cornmarket Insurance Brokers. A website with links to the ASTI website was established in 2007. The increased membership led to a much more varied social agenda not only with an increase in branch coffee-mornings but also with organised trips both within Ireland and overseas.

Cordial relations established with kindred organisations, particularly with retired teacher groups such as those representing the INTO, TUI, IFUT and NASUWT. The National Committee established relations with the Irish Senior Citizens' Parliament (ISCP), the National Federation of Pensioners' Associations (NFPA) and the Retired Workers Committee of the ICTU. Through these organisations it kept a watching brief on the many changes that were being imposed on pension rights and entitlements in the early years of the new millennium. Members of the National Committee also made visits to regional branches to assist in their formation and continuation and Sarah Scott, Catherine McHugh and Nuala O'Connor were particularly active in this aspect of the Committee's work.

The Limerick Branch submitted five motions to the Annual General Meeting in 2006. The motions were principally concerned with organisational matters. The branch submitted a further five motions to the 2007 AGM, which were also concerned with organisational matters. These were duly adopted. Three further motions were submitted by the Wicklow Branch. One of these stated "That all officers ideally serve a period of office of two years. No officer should be elected for more than two consecutive periods without a break."[163] All motions were adopted but it was becoming increasingly obvious that the Rules and Constitution of the RSTA would have to be revised and adapted to take account of the changing circumstances and the increase in membership that was taking place outside the Dublin area. This work was entrusted to the Limerick branch. Speaking at a meeting of the national Committee on 9th April 2008 the RSTA president Louis O'Flaherty congratulated Dáithí Geary and the Limerick members for their work on the proposed new constitution. He suggested that the draft should be printed and sent to members. There was a preliminary discussion on the draft document and it was agreed that under the revised constitution that no officer should serve more than three consecutive years in office.[164]

An Extraordinary General Meeting to approve and adopt the new constitution was held in the South Court Hotel, Limerick on 4th February 2009. The delegates were welcomed to Limerick by Lelia Fitzgerald, Chairperson of the Limerick Branch and the meeting was chaired by the recently elected President of the RSTA, Marie Doyle. Nearly all the changes proposed were of a technical nature and as there had been widespread consultation before the EGM only minor changes were made to the draft proposals on the day. The result was that at the conclusion of the business the RSTA was equipped with a new set of Rules and a Constitution to suit the changed needs of the organisation. The draft Rules agreed in Limerick were finally adopted at the AGM on 6th May 2009.

Both Louis O'Flaherty, President, and Catherine McHugh, Treasurer, stepped down from their respective honorary positions at the 2008 AGM.[165] In his final address O'Flaherty said that it was important that the RSTA should remain independent of the ASTI while still maintaining friendly relations with it.[166] This was a clear indication that he did not favour the restructuring of the RSTA as a branch of the ASTI, especially with the very limited representation which had been proposed in the documents prepared by Pat King some years earlier. O'Flaherty went on to say that the RSTA should be as inclusive as possible and that unlike the ASTI the RSTA was prepared to admit retired religious to the membership. Marie Doyle was elected President and Dáithí Geary, who had done considerable work on the preparation of the revised constitution was elected Vice-President. Eileen Kelly was elected Secretary and Sarah Scott, a former RSTA President was elected Treasurer. They did not know it but they were assuming office at a very critical time not only for the RSTA but for the financial wellbeing of the country.

During the early months of 2008 it was becoming increasingly obvious that what had become popularly known as the "Celtic Tiger" was on its last legs. The coup de grace was delivered on 30th September 2008 when the Government issued a bank guarantee in order to save Irish banks from collapse. This was quickly followed by an austerity programme as the Government engaged in a bid to save money wherever it could. One of the first proposals was to withdraw the universal entitlement to a medical card from all those over seventy years of age. This met with an unexpected outcry from the public. The RSTA hastily acquired a large banner and joined the mass protest outside Leinster House on 22nd October 2008. The Government and the general public were amazed at the turnout of more than 15,000 mainly elderly people. The Government reacted swiftly and introduced the Health Act, 2008, which removed the automatic entitlement to a medical card for the over 70s and introduced a means test. The means test level was generous but it did create a precedent where it could be further reduced in future years. The original income limit for an over 70 medical card was set at a gross €600 per week for a single person or €1,200 for a couple.

All of this was acknowledged in Marie Doyle's presidential address at the RSTA AGM in 2009. She said that the RSTA had participated in numerous protests against education cutbacks and massive job losses. She said that the young and the old were the targets of the cutbacks. She further said that a most disturbing feature of recent events was the ongoing attack on public sector workers and that there seemed to be a campaign to set private sector workers against public sector workers. She said that the Government, the employers and the media were involved in a campaign of scapegoating while the real culprits were enjoying large salaries, inflated bonuses and pensions. It was a striking rallying address the like of which had not been heard at an RSTA meeting for a long time. She concluded by quoting Edmund Burke "There is a limit at which forebearance ceases to be a virtue."[167] These sentiments were ably endorsed by fraternal delegates Denis Desmond RTA, Christy Conville RTUI, Margaret Murray NASUWT and Sylvia Meehan, President of the Senior Citizens' Parliament.

Because of the ongoing levies and cuts being imposed on public sector workers due to the austerity measures being introduced by the Government it was decided to seek a formal meeting with the ASTI to apprise the union of matters relating to the RSTA. This was deemed necessary because while the RSTA could participate in protests and demonstrations it did not have any negotiating rights either with the Government or the ICTU. The meeting with John White, General Secretary ASTI and Pat Hurley, President ASTI took place in Tomás McDonagh House (the ASTI Head Office) on 1st July 2009. The RSTA delegates were Marie Doyle, Nuala O'Connor and Louis O'Flaherty. The RSTA delegates stressed the good relations, which existed between the two organisations and the fact that the RSTA had supported the ASTI in recent demonstrations. John White acknowledged this. The RSTA delegates asked to have a representative attend all ASTI pre-retirement meetings to encourage retiring teachers to join the RSTA. They further requested that a staff member in ASTI Head Office would be given a specific function to deal with retired members. While White was amenable to the former request in response to the latter he said that while he was sympathetic to the request there was no possibility that a person would be appointed. Staff members had been reduced in

Head Office but any officer there was capable of dealing with problems that might arise.[168]

John White attended a meeting of the National Committee on 28th January 2010 and informed the members that the Government had made a decision to raise the retirement age of teachers to 66. This was in stark contrast to the terms, which had been available under the PCW, which had allowed retirement in certain circumstances at 55 years. He further stated that in the future pensions would be calculated on a career average rather than salary at point of retirement. This would mean that future pensions would be less generous. He also said that it was proposed to break the link between the salaries of serving teachers and pensioners and that future increases would most likely be based on the consumer price index (CPI).[169]

Members of the committee expressed dismay at the information given by White. Sarah Scott said that it would be a good idea to retain parity even if it meant a decrease of 6% or 7% in pensions. Other members said that every effort should be made to resist any break between the salaries of serving teachers and the pensions paid to retired members. There was a need to alert young teachers to the importance of pensions and that attempts to divide and conquer members of the teaching profession should be resisted.[170]

A meeting between representatives of the RSTA, INTO Retired and TUI Retired was held on 9th February 2010 to discuss how they could co-operate with each other and with their respective unions to safeguard their pension entitlements. The meeting was of an exploratory nature and it was agreed that a further meeting would take place on 20th April, after the annual conferences of the teachers unions, all of which were to debate motions on pension parity.[171] In the event that meeting did not take place and the two motions on pensions which were due to be debated at the ASTI Annual Convention in Galway were not taken due to pressure of other business.[172]

Feelings of anger and annoyance were expressed at the Annual General Meeting of the RSTA on 5th May 2010. Marie Doyle, in her Presidential Address, decried the Government policies, which were set to reduce pensions and lower standards of living and to renege on existing contracts of employment. She said that in her opinion legitimate expectations only extended to politicians, bankers and judges.

She said she was annoyed at the constant reference in the media to public sector workers as parasites living off the Irish taxpayers. Her comments were endorsed by fraternal delegates from the retired sections of the INTO, TUI, IFUT and NASUWT together with Sylvia Meehan of the Senior Citizens' Parliament.[173]

While the terms and conditions for the payment of secondary school teachers' pensions had been changed on a frequent basis since 1995, there had been no attempt to reduce the pensions of retired teachers. But in March 2009 a levy of approximately 7.5% was imposed on all public sector pensioners and at the same time a moratorium was placed on the appointment of serving teachers to posts of responsibility. Within the RSTA there was a feeling of regret that the two motions on pensions, which were scheduled for debate at the ASTI Annual Convention in 2010 had not been debated. There was also a sense of hurt because some delegates to the Convention in Galway had been critical of retired teachers who were taking part-time or substitution work which could be undertaken by younger unemployed teachers. There were signs of a growing divide between serving teachers and those who had already retired. This divide was clearly demonstrated in an article by Joe Coy in ASTIR where he criticised retired teachers for supervising state examinations.[174] Coy's contention was that by doing this work retired members were depriving younger teachers of much needed income. Coy referred to retired teachers as "have beens" and also suggested that retired teachers may have been prioritised for this work so that there would be no interruption to the state examinations in the event of industrial action by teachers. There was considerable annoyance in the RSTA not only at the content of the Coy article but at the fact that it had been published in ASTIR while an article on pensions, which had been previously submitted to ASTIR had its publication delayed for over a year.[175]

It was decided to write to the Editorial Board of ASTIR about the matter[176] and in the Christmas RSTA Newsletter there was a rebuttal of the Coy article by Louis O'Flaherty. O'Flaherty took exception to the inference that retired teachers might act as strike breakers and said that there was documentary evidence of RSTA members standing shoulder to shoulder with their striking colleagues in every industrial dispute since 1964. He said that the RSTA had urged its members not to engage in substitution work where younger teachers were available but that it could not force them to comply with its recommendations. He also stated that money earned supervising State examinations should never be a substitute for a decent salary for young teachers.[177]

Following the collapse of the Irish banking system and the Irish economy in 2008 a series of financial cutbacks had been introduced by the Fianna Fáil led Government. Cutbacks continued under the Fine Gael/Labour Government after its election in early 2011. The collapse of the Celtic Tiger led to massive unemployment and the media became highly critical of the public service notwithstanding the cutbacks, which were being imposed on its members. There was evidence of a growing divide between public and private sector employees. Government policy, which had created lower pay scales for new entrants to the teaching profession caused rancour and became a major issue within the teacher trade unions. The pensions' issue slipped further down the priority list. It was in this context that the RSTA sought a meeting with senior officers of the ASTI. There had been a growing feeling in the RSTA that the ASTI, despite its generous subvention and commitment, was becoming less interested in matters relating to retired members. This feeling was allayed somewhat at the AGM of the RSTA on 4th May 2011 when Pat King, General Secretary ASTI acknowledged the work which had been done in the past by ASTI members who were now retired. He said that the ASTI and the RSTA were facing very difficult times and that they shared many common interests. He reminded the RSTA that the ASTI had got legal advice regarding pension cuts after the RSTA had requested it but unfortunately the advice given was that the Government could do almost anything it chose to do by way of emergency legislation. He did suggest that a more formal relationship between the two organisations might be mutually beneficial. He said that a motion to Annual Convention on "emeritus" members of the ASTI had been badly phrased. He said that there was no plan to introduce a subscription for "emeritus" members but that it seemed inappropriate that retired teachers should have a vote on the conditions of work enjoyed by serving teachers. He did, however, accept that it was appropriate that retired members should serve on some committees, particularly the Pensions Sub-Committee but that these issues would merit further discussion.[178]

While at the AGM there was a general feeling of fraternal solidarity, the mood would seem to have changed by the time the formal meeting between the two Officer boards occurred later in the year. At that meeting the ASTI was represented by General Secretary Pat King, President Brendan Broderick, Vice President Gerry Breslin and Honorary Treasurer Ray St. John. The RSTA was represented by President Henry

Collins, Immediate Past President Marie Doyle, Honorary Secretary Seán Fallon and Honorary Treasurer Muriel McNicholas. The RSTA delegation got the distinct feeling that the ASTI regarded matters relating to retired members as peripheral to the core issues facing the union and that "The ASTI focus is on serving teachers, not retirees."[179] The ASTI officers expressed the view that retired members were exerting an undue influence in the branches of the union and that it was inappropriate that retired members should vote on the pay and conditions of serving teachers. The officers further indicated a desire to see separate branches established for ASTI "emeritus" members.[180] They did, however, say that a new staff member, Desmond O'Toole had been employed who would deal with pensions and related issues. The feeling among the RSTA members was that they did not wish to have a separate branch structure for "emeritus" members. Even if they were in favour of such a proposal they could not speak for all "emeritus" members for while most RSTA members were "emeritus" members not all "emeritus" members were members of the RSTA.

The relationship between the ASTI and the RSTA was discussed at further meetings of the RSTA National Committee. Carmel Heneghan, who was also a member of the ASTI Equal Opportunities Committee, outlined her feelings on the report of the discussion with the ASTI officers and the content of some of the motions at the 2011 ASTI Annual Convention. She said that the proposed changes, where age (retirement) is so central to the difference in rights amounted to ageism and that such changes would be a retrograde step for the ASTI since it would reduce access to the strengths of the retired members.[181] It was also felt that the number of retired members attending ASTI Annual Convention could be limited by introducing a quota system for branches.

The feeling within the RSTA that the interests of retired members were not being actively pursued by the parent union was also being felt by the retired members in other public sector unions. In September 2011 a new group representing retired public sector workers was formed. The Alliance of Retired Public Servants (ARPS) was established for the purpose of providing a united front for the protection of public sector pensions. One of the prime movers in this organisation was Christy Conville, Secretary of the Retired Members Association- Teachers' Union of Ireland. While the primary motive for the establishment of the Alliance was the protection of pension entitlements it is also concerned with the retention of benefits required by older people such as personal health, social services and travel facilities. RSTA members Marie Doyle, Mike Moriarty, Susie Hall, Carmel Heneghan and Phil O'Doherty continue to be active within the Alliance.

Speaking at the RSTA AGM on 2nd May 2012 Henry Collins, President, said "The unilateral reduction in remuneration for 2011 entrants to the teaching service and the cap on qualification allowances constitute a direct undermining of the status of teachers that could only be to the detriment of teaching in the longer term".[182] He went on to say that the cuts marked a return to the days of two teaching scales, one for women and single men and the other, more favourable one for married men. They marked a return to the days of the Specialist Teachers who were employed under different conditions than general subject teachers. He further said that the RSTA would support their serving colleagues in their campaign "to secure just and equitable treatment for new entrants to the teaching profession.[183] The Annual General Meeting went on to adopt a motion expressing its dismay at the threat to discontinue payment of qualification allowances to newly qualified teachers.[184] The fact that the RSTA was limited in the extent of its support for young teachers was indicative of its own position. The RSTA has no negotiating rights on behalf of its members and must depend on the goodwill of its parent body. Retired teachers cannot take industrial action but they can be supportive of those who are still at the "chalkface."

The 2012 AGM was a high point of the RSTA as it marked the fiftieth anniversary of its foundation. It was held over two days in the Granville Hotel in Waterford and was hosted by members of the local branch led by its Chairperson, John Cunningham. While it was not the first AGM to be held outside Dublin, (that honour went to Galway in 1984) it was the first that involved two nights in a hotel, which contributed in no small way to the bonding of the membership. Muriel McNicholas, RSTA Honorary National Treasurer was able to announce that the finances of the association were in good shape and that the membership stood at just under fourteen hundred, organised in sixteen branches throughout the country. It was a far cry from the plea from George Lodge at the 1967 AGM when he reflected that it would be nice if they could afford to have a little standing buffet on that one night of the year.

Apart from the celebration of the fiftieth anniversary of its foundation the RSTA launched its new newsletter format, commissioned a new logo and established a very professional website. All this was undertaken not only to keep members informed but also to reinforce a recruitment drive. An increase in membership had become increasingly desirable if not essential. The Department of Education and Skills had written to the RSTA in June 2012 stating that its continued operation of the deduction of subscriptions at source (DAS) from the Retired Teachers Payroll was dependant on ten-percent of the relevant payroll participating. Unfortunately that percentage had not been reached despite the increase in membership. Just under eighty-percent of subscriptions came through the mandate system and to collect subscriptions in any other way would be both troublesome and expensive.[185] The RSTA had sought and received help from the ASTI in seeking a postponement of the DES directive.

It is to be hoped that the RSTA will continue to receive support from the ASTI in its recruitment drive, notwithstanding the difficulties being encountered by the parent body in securing proper working conditions for its serving members.

CHAPTER 10:
SOCIAL AND CULTURAL ACTIVITIES

The early years of the RSTA were notable for their almost total absence of social activities. The association had been formed primarily for the pursuit of a just pension scheme for retired secondary teachers, with the aspiration that they would one day achieve pension parity with their working colleagues. The core group was very small and its members were all in their late sixties.

When George Lodge delivered his presidential speech at the fifth AGM of the RSTA on 22nd March 1967 he concluded by saying "it would be nice if they could afford to have a little standing buffet for this one night and meet one another on a more social footing." There is no evidence extant of such an event happening but no doubt there was a feeling of collegiality at the meetings and one suspects that there may have been some social activity even if it only comprised of going for a drink after a meeting. It was not until Dónal Ó Conalláin became President that social activity became an intrinsic element of the RSTA. At a meeting in Liberty Hall, Dublin in November 1981 Tomás Ó Riain proposed that "some kind of a social should be held, clear of association matters to enable members to meet in a friendly atmosphere."[186] This was the second meeting of the RSTA following its restructuring after a particularly acrimonious period.

It was decided that the next AGM would be held in Power's Hotel, Dublin on 24th March 1982 at 11.30.am. and to have lunch at 1.30.pm. The notification included the cryptic comment "members will, of course, be responsible for their own nutritional expenses."[187] It would seem that the lunch was a success and a presentation was made to Máire MacDonagh on her impending retirement as General Secretary of the ASTI after 25 years. it was decided to hold a dinner in the same hotel on Friday 22nd October 1982. This was to be the first Annual dinner of the RSTA and the overall charge (to include wines) was £10.00. The principal organisers of the function were Mona Hughes and Tomás Ó Riain. There was an attendance of forty, most of whom were from the Dublin area but the former treasurer of the ASTI, Vera Blake and her sister travelled from Armagh.[188] It was decided to hold the AGM in Power's Hotel on 23rd March 1983, to be followed by lunch.

It was decided to hold the 1984 Annual Dinner in Power's Hotel but before the venue was finally agreed there was some discussion about the provision of a piano in the hotel. As arrangements were being made it became apparent that there was no piano in the hotel and that it would cost £60 to £65 to hire one. It was agreed that a piano would be hired provided it did not cost more than £30.[189] The minutes are silent as to how the matter was resolved but the Annual Dinner was held in Power's Hotel on 5th October 1984. A very pleasant evening was had and after dinner "vocal cords were strained in renditions of an assortment of songs varying from the ribald to the pietistic. The pianist, Ellie Cole, dealt very competently with all variations - and so to the witching hour and Auld Lang Syne."[190]

Both Tomás Ó Riain and Dónal Ó Conalláin were keen advocates of the building of a social dimension in the RSTA. After the 1984 Annual Dinner the National Committee, which in many ways was indistinguishable from the Dublin Committee, decided to hold coffee mornings in Wynn's Hotel, Dublin every month and it was hoped that Galway and Cork members would follow the example set by Dublin.[191] After a few months it was decided to re-locate the coffee mornings from Wynn's Hotel to the Royal Dublin Hotel, to be held on the first Wednesday of every month at 11.am.[192]

The 1985 Annual Dinner was again held in Power's Hotel, Dublin and was widely reported in the October issue of ASTIR, with numerous photographs of the attendees. The ASTI was represented by Michael Ward, National Treasurer of the ASTI, who was always supportive of the RSTA.

On 27th November 1985 the RSTA had a Mass celebrated in St. Kevin's Oratory, Marlborough St., Dublin for the repose of the souls of deceased members of the RSTA. The celebrant was Fr. Brendan Kearney S.J., a son of Bert Kearney, a recently deceased member of the RSTA and frequent contributor to Dublin Opinion and other journals. The annual Mass in November was to become a feature of RSTA activities for a number of years and was to be subsequently taken up by the Cork Branch. In more recent times it has been replaced by a moment of reflection at the Annual General Meeting.

During the 1980s and the 1990s the principal social functions of the RSTA were the Annual General Meetings, which were held outside Dublin in alternate years, the Annual Dinner, usually based in Dublin, the Dublin Coffee Mornings and the Annual mass for deceased members.

At a Committee meeting in June 1992 Maureen Lynch suggested that an approach should be made to USIT to try and get reduced air travel for members and it was agreed that the secretary, Maeve Colbert would make enquiries in that regard.[193] At the following meeting Nora Kelleher suggested that social outings should be undertaken and that some of the cost should be paid individually and that the remainder should be met from central funds. She was supported by other members in this proposal.[194] The 1993 Annual General Meeting was held in Hayes' Hotel, Thurles and was followed by a visit to Holy Cross Abbey were Archbishop Morris acted as guide and explained the history and restoration of the abbey.[195] On 1st June 1994 the Dublin contingent of the RSTA had a guided tour of Newman House, St. Stephen's Green, Dublin and this was followed up in June 1995 with a visit to the newly refurbished Government offices in Merrion Street, Dublin, followed by lunch in the National Gallery.[196]

As noted elsewhere the mid-nineties became a period of turmoil within the RSTA involving heated debate and discussion about pension parity, the PCW and the proposal to re-establish the RSTA as a branch within the ASTI. The coffee mornings continued as did the Annual Dinner and some social events occurred around the AGM but other organised social events ceased for a time although individual branches did have local social activities. In 2000 the Dublin coffee mornings relocated from the Royal Dublin Hotel to the Teachers' Club in Parnell Square. This move was brought about by the Royal Dublin Hotel seeking a charge of £100 for the room while the Teachers' Club was prepared to offer its facilities for £40.[197] The Dublin Branch continues to meet in the Teachers' Club on the first Wednesday of the month. The Dublin Branch arranged for outings to Farmleigh, Ayrefield House and Dublin Castle in 2002.[198] Other branches also organised outings and lectures. The Cork Branch had initiated coffee mornings in the Ambassador Hotel and also arranged for a programme of classical music to be presented by Mr. Séamus Murphy. The Galway Branch had a talk on iconography given by Pauline Gillan while the Limerick Branch had a lecture on The Changing Face of Limerick, given by the city Engineer Séamus O'Sullivan. The Wicklow branch made a group visit to the National Concert hall for a performance of the Pirates of Penzance.[199] The Mayo Branch paid a visit to the Country Life Museum near Castlebar on 5th February 2002 and subsequently visited the Victorian Gardens at Kylemore. Three new branches were established in 2002. The Wexford Branch held its inaugural meeting in the Talbot Hotel, Wexford on 21st February and the new Kerry Branch held its first meeting in the Killarney Court Hotel on 26th February 2002. The newly formed Tipperary Branch had its first meeting at the County Museum on 27th February.[200]

Outings and social events were not confined to the members of a particular branch but were open to all members and they have increased in number and diversity over recent years.[201] The first overseas visit by the RSTA was organised in 2002 when a group went to Fuengirola in October, which was followed the following year by a visit to Kitzbuhel in Austria.[202] In 2005 Louis O'Flaherty led a group to New York while Eileen Brennan organised a trip to Slovenia. The North East Branch organised a trip to the battlefields of Europe in 2007 followed by a visit to Barcelona in the Spring of 2007. Following the success of the 2005 visit a further group of 20 members undertook a visit to New York in May 2008. In October 2009 a group from the Kildare Branch undertook the Camino in Northern Spain to the shrine of St. James at Santiago de Compostella. In September 2010 a group of members from the Cork Branch travelled to Salzburg, Bechtesgaden and Oberammergau while the North East Branch was content with a visit to Cavan and Fermanagh with a stopover at the Marble Arch Caves. In 2012 a group from the Midlands Branch visited Moscow and St. Petersburg. Most social and cultural activities are now organised at a local branch level but all members are encouraged to participate in any of the activities they desire. Branch meetings are regularly held and these are advertised in the Newsletter and on the new website.

The extent and scope of the social and cultural activities undertaken and enjoyed by the branches has greatly expanded and can be better comprehended by reading the reports of the various branches in the next chapter.

The Social and Cultural Relationship with the NASUWT

In April 2002 Gerry Campbell, Secretary of the NASUWT (Retired), having seen the RSTA page in the ASTIR magazine, wrote to Nuala O'Connor, then National Secretary, suggesting that some sort of liaison and sharing of ideas might be of benefit to both groups. This proposal, which was eagerly taken up by the National Committee, was later described by Gerry Campbell as an example of "stretching out a hand across the now non-existent border." The following October five members from each group met in Ballymascanlon. RSTA members at that first meeting were Eileen Brennan, Nuala Carroll, Catherine McHugh, Tomás MacCathmhaoil RIP and Nuala O'Connor. On the Belfast side were Gerry Campbell, Lottie Ewing, Jack Eaton, Jean Thompson and Earl Preston. There was an immediate rapport between the two delegations and plans were made for an exchange of visits, north and south.

The following February, thirty one NASUWT members travelled by train and car, braving very snowy conditions to attend the Dublin Branch's meeting in the Teachers' Club, Parnell Square, where they were warmly welcomed and then listened to a presentation by Ted Courtenay of Baroque, Classical and Romantic music.

The first journey north took place in June that year, when twenty four Dublin and Wicklow members went to Belfast for a boat trip on the Lagan. It was such a pleasure for the visitors to sail along the river through a peaceful Belfast, enjoying the tea and coffee thoughtfully brought on board by the Belfast group. These first visits formed a template for all subsequent outings. Visits always include a meal together where the conversation is as often about family, especially grandchildren, as about history or politics. Outings are well attended with numbers at times reaching sixty or even seventy.

There have been visits to places of cultural or historical interest in Belfast, Dublin and places in between such as Armagh, Drogheda, Tara, Trim Castle and Glencree Reconciliation Centre with its record of peace-making in connection with the Northern Troubles.

In Belfast there were joint visits to Cultra Folk and Transport Museum, to City Hall, the Ulster Hall, the newly refurbished Ulster Museum and to a catering college where the historian, Jonathan Bardon gave an interesting talk on the history of Belfast. Highlights of these outings were a visit to the excellent Titanic Exhibition in June 2012 and in 2008 a visit to Stormont. At the latter, after a tour of the building, the groups were welcomed by Mervyn Stokey, MLA, Chair of the Education Committee who showed a great interest in the continuing friendship between the two organisations.

The Belfast Operatic Company presents a musical each year in which NASUWT members are involved, both on stage and behind the scenes. RSTA members attend these and have enjoyed excellent performances in musicals ranging from "Hello Dolly" and "Orpheus in the Underworld" to "Titanic, the Musical" in 2012.

In Dublin, major events included a visit to the Dáil in session, a reception in the Mansion House by the Lord Mayor, Emer Costello and a visit to Áras an Úachtaráin. At the latter event sixty people were received by the President, Mary McAleese, to whom a painting of Rostrevor was presented by artist, George Stainer on behalf of both groups. Among other places visited were Arbour Hill, Croke Park, Kilmainham Gaol and the War Memorial in Islandbridge. Louis O'Flaherty, led walking tours around medieval and Georgian Dublin. One of these tours ended with a visit to the Bank of Ireland, Foster Place, formerly the House of Parliament. This had a particular resonance for the groups as they listened to an audio version of the debate on the Act of Union in 1800 and afterwards in the old House of Lords, viewed two tapestries depicting the Defence of Derry and the Battle of the Boyne.

Both organisations send representatives who speak at their respective AGMs and at celebrations such as anniversaries and Christmas lunches. At the RSTA AGM in 2003 the first they attended, Thompie Steele, Social Secretary of the NASUWT group greatly enlivened proceedings by singing to his own guitar accompaniment "Lord in his mercy, be kind to Belfast."

The Wicklow Branch joined with the Dublin Branch in organising these events. Wicklow Secretary, Aveen Kilduff organised the trip to Glencree and Powerscourt. Other branches also organised exchanges, notably the North-East Branch led by Michael McMahon. In 2007 Michael organised a guided tour of the Patrick

Kavanagh country ending in Creggan churchyard in South Armagh and, in 2009 led members back in history in a fascinating tour around the Cooley Peninsula and the Táin trail. The Mayo and Cork Branches have also entertained the Northern group in their respective counties and the Kilkenny Branch gave a reception to the visiting RSTA and NASUWT members at the River Court Hotel followed by a guided tour of their beautiful city.

From tentative beginnings the link with the NASUWT (retired) has gone from strength to strength. Friendships have flourished and a greater insight into the history and cultural diversity of the country has been fostered. The groups celebrated their ten years of friendship in October 2012 in a tour of the Battle of the Boyne Heritage Centre. The exhibits there, and the talks by the excellent guides, gave the visitors a far better understanding of this famous battle by placing it in its wider European context.

David Mehaffey, President of the NASUWT group commented that he could not think of a more appropriate setting in which to celebrate the first ten years of friendship and cooperation between members of our associations. He went on to say "Let us look forward to spending more sunny days together with glasses always at least half-full."

CHAPTER 11:
THE BRANCHES

Clare	Cork	Donegal
Dublin	Galway	Kerry
Kildare	Kilkenny	Limerick
Mayo	Midlands	North East
Sligo	Tipperary	Waterford
Wexford	Wicklow	

Clare Branch

The Clare Branch is the seventeenth and most recently formed branch of the RSTA. It owes its genesis to a number of casual meetings, which a number of retired secondary teachers in the Ennis area had in the West County and Templegate hotels in 2012. As a result an explanatory meeting about establishing a branch in Clare was held with members of the Galway and Limerick branches. Following these meetings it was decided that a branch should be formed. The Clare Branch was formally constituted at a meeting in the Templegate Hotel on 30th January 2013. It was formally launched by the Vice-President of the RSTA, Carmel Heneghan. Two of the founder members, Michael Corley and Jack Keane are former presidents of the ASTI. A programme of activities is already being organised. The Chairperson is Helen Meade and the Honorary Secretary is Mary Carroll. Kathleen Pyne is the Treasurer and also on the committee are Mary Hayes and Nora Liddy.

Cork Branch

In late 1997 two retired members of the ASTI, Tom Walshe and Humphrey Twomey decided to try to establish a branch of the RSTA in Cork. It was a particularly troubled time in the RSTA but the two persisted and called a meeting of interested parties. Others present at the inaugural meeting were Pat Browne, Pat Healy, Tony Burke, Seán Kenny and Ann Mullane. Tom Walshe became the first Chairman. It was decided, initially, to meet formally on the third Thursday of the month during school term. The original topic of discussion was the changed pension arrangements resulting from the Programme for Competitiveness and Work but members soon realised that they could do little to influence these matters as they lacked negotiating powers and as a result the social element grew in importance. The early meetings were held in premises at 32 South Terrace but when these premises were sold the venue moved to the Parish Centre of the Sacred Heart Church on Western Road. Many of the meetings are still held there but in recent years it has been decided to augment these meetings with coffee mornings in the Ambassador Hotel, Military Hill at 11.am. on the first Wednesday of each month during school term.

Some events have become traditional in the branch over the years. A gramophone recital by Séamus Murphy is held every autumn. In late November or early December there is a commemorative Mass for deceased members followed by a Christmas lunch. This is usually the best-attended function of the year and the branch has always been happy to welcome members of other branches to that occasion. Some years ago it was decided to move that function to Ballincollig, which is outside the city, but it has not proved to be as successful as was hoped for and it is now being considered to move back within the city. In May the branch usually undertakes a day coach trip to a place of interest, which also includes a lunch in a local restaurant. Places visited on these outings have included the battle site at Kinsale, guided by Tom Walshe. Visits have been undertaken to Holy Cross Abbey, Glenstal, Lismore Castle, Glin, Mizzen Head and the National Stud in Kildare. Many of these were organised by Pat Browne. In 2010 a small group undertook a trip to Oberammergau, Munich, Vienna and Salzburg.

When not travelling around, lectures and talks have been organised on such diverse subjects as art and literature, military history, politics, credit unions, missionary work, gardening and technology, given by Tim Cramer, Tom Dunne, Bridget Coughlan, Alicia St. Leger, Pat Gunn, Humphrey Twomey, Tony Clifford and Charlie Wilkins.

One of the more interesting and colourful characters associated with the Cork branch was Seán Lydon. Lydon had spent most of his teaching career in Christian Brothers' College and for 36 years he contributed a column to the Southern Star under the pen name J.J. He was much admired for his ascerbic style and inimitable perspicacity. He was very popular at the RSTA meetings and his presence was guaranteed to enliven any meeting of the RSTA or the ASTI. His lecture on journalism, which was given to the branch, was probably the best attended of all the RSTA meetings in Cork. Unfortunately he died in April 2002 and was remembered with affection at the Annual General Meeting of the RSTA on 8th May 2002.

The present committee consists of Treasa Healy, Chairperson, Pat Spillane, Vice Chairperson, Nuala Buckley, Honorary Secretary, Liam Long, Assistant Secretary and Mary Hurley, Honorary Treasurer, together with Pat Honohan and Pat Browne.[203]

Donegal Branch

The Donegal branch of the RSTA was set up in April 2010 at the request of several retired teachers who got in touch with the national organisation. The inaugural meeting took place in the Clanree Hotel, Letterkenny and was attended by Marie Doyle who was the National President and by Sarah Scott who was National Treasurer at the time. An excellent turn out demonstrated a high level of interest in establishing a branch of the RSTA within the county and so this was followed up very shortly afterwards with another meeting to elect officers and prepare a preliminary programme of events.

At that meeting the following board of officers was elected: Gerard Logue, Chairperson, June Hosty, Secretary and Adrienne Browne, Treasurer. The formalities of opening a branch bank account were attended to and recruitment of new members began. There was some discussion as to how to develop contact with members and it was decided to set up a blog and email account. The meeting also agreed to contact everybody either by SMS or email about regular meetings. This system has worked really well and has the advantage of being very economical.

It was also decided to meet regularly on the first Wednesday of each month at 11.30.a.m. and to have lunch after the formal business of the branch would be completed. Old habits die hard - the branch still observes the academic calendar!

No meetings are held in the summer months, June, July and August or in January as most members have other commitments to attend to at these times. The venue in that first year was the Clanree Hotel where a very favourable price was negotiated for an excellent lunch. It was also agreed to try to organise some social event in addition to the regular meeting each month.

Since its formation the branch has been on visits to the Dáil and the Northern Ireland Assembly and has undertaken guided tours of Derry and the National Park in Glenveagh as well as organising some very pleasant visits to the local theatre and supporting other cultural events locally. These occasions are usually preceded by visits to excellent local restaurants.

In 2010-2011 the same officers were re-elected and the meeting place was switched to the Grianán Theatre, Letterkenny, where the Green Room is available as a meeting room for branch deliberations. The theatre also has a restaurant, so the tradition of long relaxing lunches continues.

There are difficulties associated with organising meetings in a very scattered county like Donegal and the severe winters caused attendances to fall off at times. Nevertheless, there are in excess of 30 active members and there is great enthusiasm for the RSTA among the recently retired. A new committee for 2012-2013 was elected in September 2012 as follows: Chairperson, Carmel Dunleavy, Secretary, Gerard Logue and Treasurer, Nuala Flynn. The branch hopes to have representatives attend the annual general meeting of the National Association in May 2013.[204]

Dublin Branch

The RSTA was founded in Dublin and in its early years there were few members outside the capital. Real expansion outside of Dublin began in the late 90s and it was then that the concept of branches other than Dublin began to arise. Most of the members of the National Committee were Dublin based so there was no clear demarcation between the Dublin members and the National organisation. In recent years the Dublin branch has assumed a separate identity. Regular meetings and talks/lectures are held on the first Wednesday of the month in the Teachers' Club, Parnell Square. Topics raised and discussed have been varied and include astronomy, crime and punishment, falconry and Tai Chi while outings have been undertaken to

Croke Park, the Botanic Gardens and Historic Dublin walks.

Over the years a very close relationship has been built up between the Dublin branch and members of the NASUWT Retired branch in Belfast. This has led to a number of exchange visits between the two groups. These follow an initial meeting in the Ballymascanlan Hotel, Dundalk in 2002 between members of the two groups led by Nuala O'Connor, RSTA and Gerry Campbell, NASUWT. Places visited by the Dublin branch include Stormont Castle, the Titanic Experience, Cultra Folk Park and the Ulster Museum and Botanic Gardens. There have also been regular visits to musicals in the Belfast Opera House.

Until recently the Dublin branch members were responsible for the posting of the RSTA newsletters, when members would gather in the ASTI Head Office to fold and post the latest news. The traditional Christmas Lunch is held on the first Wednesday of December in Wynne's Hotel. The current officers are Mary Kenny, Chairperson, Susie Hall, Secretary and Catherine McHugh, Treasurer together with Valerie O'Neill and Maureen O'Connor.

Galway Branch

The Galway Branch was the first branch of the RSTA to be established outside of Dublin. While there had been members based outside Dublin since the 1970s they were not organised into separate branches. In 1996 Margaret Stewart was elected to the National Committee and she set about organising what she called "The Western Section" of the RSTA. The inaugural meeting was held in Rabbitte's Pub and Restaurant, Forster Street, Galway on 27th February 1997 and was attended by RSTA President, Peter Kerr and other members of the National Committee. Stewart was ably assisted by Tadhg McCrohan and Kevin Kilgarriff and they went on to organise the National AGM of the RSTA, which was held in the Great Southern Hotel, Galway on 17th April 1997. Margaret Stewart was elected Vice-President of the RSTA at that meeting. The branch held its early meetings in the Sacre Coeur Hotel where it was greatly assisted by the Dunleavy family. On the 11th April 2001 Stewart accompanied by RSTA President, Seán Geraghty and some members of the Galway Branch travelled to meet interested members in the Knockranny Hotel, Westport. As a result of that meeting the Mayo branch was formally organised in Daly's Hotel, Castlebar on the 8th October 2001 with an initial enrolment of 40 members. Apart from those already mentioned, some of the earliest office-holders were Noreen Briscoe, Maureen O'Malley, Maura Stevens and Peggy McDermott. The branch has organised the usual coffee mornings, lunches, outings and guest lectures on such diverse subjects as herbal medicine and the Boer War. There are currently 93 members and the officers are Mattie Quinn, Chairperson, Sheila Conneely, Honorary Secretary and Mary Molloy, Honorary Treasurer.

Kerry Branch

The first recorded member from Kerry was a Mrs. Scanlon who attended a National Committee meeting on 2nd May 1984. The next recorded reference to Kerry is in the minutes of the National Committee meeting of 19th February 2002 where it is noted that the new branches in Wexford, Killarney and Tipperary were discussed and whether or not all branches could be represented on the executive committee. It was decided that this would not be feasible because of numbers. Despite this setback to the nascent Kerry Branch it thrived under the stewardship of Ann Cox. Over the years the branch has been involved in numerous cultural activities. There have been such events as a talk on the establishment of Siamsa Tíre and the history of Killarney. Outings have been undertaken to Gougane Barra, Listowel and the Cliffs of Moher. There was also a regular attendance at the Christmas lunch and Mass for deceased members, which in the early years was celebrated in the Franciscan Friary in Killarney. By 2011 many of the founder members of the Kerry Branch were of advanced age and were finding it difficult to arrange branch functions. Henry Collins, President and Seán Fallon, Honorary National Secretary met with nine members of the branch and were impressed by their sense of duty and loyalty. However, these members felt they had been left to carry responsibility for the branch for a long time and they wanted new blood to take over. A meeting was arranged and 35 retired teachers attended to help re-form the branch. Some were long time members and others were new recruits. It was decided to re-start the branch with a Mass followed by lunch in the Carlton Hotel on Tuesday 5th December 2011. Fifty members attended. Since then much of the old vibrancy has returned to the branch with regular talks and outings. Retirees in the Killarney area meet every week for coffee and a lunch is planned for the Dingle area. The current Chairperson is Breda Lyons while Tim Gleeson acts as Vice-Chairperson. The Treasurer is Mairéad NíChrualaoí and the Secretary is Bláithín Ní Bhric.[205]

Kildare Branch

The first meeting of the Kildare Branch of the RSTA took place in the Osprey Hotel, Naas on 28th February 2007. Attending members included Grace Walsh, founder and Chairperson, Phil Dunning, Secretary, Eilish McCormack, Treasurer and representatives from the National Committee who have shown great support to the branch. The branch has also been fortunate from the outset in being facilitated for their meetings by Dolores Hamill and the wonderful staff at the Kildare Education Centre, where many of the meetings take place on the fourth Wednesday of every month, excluding the summer months. By 2012 the membership of the branch had risen to 55 and they are always delighted to welcome new members to the group.

Over the years members have enjoyed many outings. Some of the outings were local and others further afield. Local history events included a tour of the historic centres of both Kildare town and Naas and a visit to the Curragh Military Museum, which gave a fascinating insight into the history of the region. They learned that Charles Dickens visited the Curragh Camp and was appalled at the poverty of the women living in the area. On another occasion they attended an illustrated talk on the history of the national Stud and the Japanese Gardens, Kildare is the home of the Irish thoroughbred horse. Castlecomer Discovery Park was a fascinating discovery. It is an exhibition of the history and geology of coal mining at Castlecomer since the 1860s located on the former Wandesford Estate which also includes over 80 acres of mixed woodland, forest rails, a craft centre and a restaurant.

The branch members have also dabbled in the arts, taking a drama lessons and patronising local dramatic productions in the Riverbank, Newbridge and the Civic Theatre in Tallaght as well as in the Abbey. They have thoroughly enjoyed some thought provoking films such as "His & Hers," "Silence" and the French subtitled "Of Gods and Men." They picked up brushes and paint for an art course in Newtownbarry House in Bunclody, County Wexford, organised by Mary Cameron. In addition, they have viewed the oriental drawings and art in the Chester Beatty Library in Dublin.

The green-fingered members took a trip to the Mount Usher Gardens; the sheltered linear garden along the Dargle River in Ashford, which has a stunning azalea walk and many rare specimen trees. They joined up with the Dublin Branch for a walk in the Liberties, led by Louis O'Flaherty and greatly enjoyed his insightful account of the area's past history.

They have also put up mileage on foot, walking to St. Brigid's Well on the Curragh, and undertaking a walk around Howth Head. Some members have also participated in the longest walk of all, the Camino. Phil Dunning, Margaret Aspel and Eilish McCormack gave the Dublin Branch an illustrated account of their walk to the shrine of St. James of Compostela in Santiago in north western Spain.

Over the years their Christmas lunches have attracted great support from members and their partners and they are looking forward to many more not only with their current members but also with the new members which they hope to recruit.[206]

Kilkenny Branch

At a meeting of the National Committee of the RSTA on 19th April 2000 it was decided that attempts should be made to establish regional branches in Limerick, Kilkenny and Wexford. The urgency of the proposal was emphasised at a further meeting on 20th September but it was noted at the meeting of 20th March 2001 that the Kilkenny branch had been firmly established and that eight members had been enrolled. The principal organiser of the Kilkenny branch was Kay Sheehy, widow of former ASTI President Alf Sheehy. Among the founding members of the branch were two former ASTI presidents, Liam Hogan and Paddy Gilman, ably assisted by Mary Grace, Paul Glennon and Joan Ryan. They were given helpful advice from Sarah Scott, Nuala Carroll and Eileen Brennan from the National Committee who travelled to Kilkenny to assist in the organisation. One of the earliest social activities was a golf outing on Wednesday 27th February 2002, which was followed by a joint meeting and lunch with members of the Wicklow Branch at Hunter's Lodge, Mount Juliet in May 2002. That visit was reciprocated with a visit and lunch at Woodenbridge hotel, Vale of Avoca on 16th October. The social element quickly developed with lunches in the Newpark Hotel and at Rathwood Home and Garden Centre. In the early years there were not too many retired teachers in the county and the meetings of the branch were often attended by members from adjoining counties such as Laois, Wexford, Carlow, Waterford and Tipperary. The early meetings took place in the Club House Hotel in Kilkenny.

Over the years the branch has had a variety of talks, lectures and outings. There have been visits to Altamont Gardens and Woodstook Gardens in Inistioge. There have been visits to the National Museum at Collins Barracks, Dublin and the Discovery Park at Castlecomer, where great interest was expressed in the geological history of the Castlecomer Coal Mines and the social history of the Wandesfort family.

While Kay Sheehy admits that the branch has been a bit less active in recent times it is hoped that with the arrival of new and younger retirees the branch will recover its former vigour with Anne Murphy, Treasurer, keeping an eye on the finances.[207]

Limerick Branch

The Limerick Branch of the RSTA was established in 1999 when a group of retired teachers held their first meeting in Hanratty's Hotel. The founding officers were Tim Frawley, Chairperson, Geraldine Reddan, Honorary Secretary and Anne Bradshaw, Treasurer. It was decided that the meetings would take place on the first Wednesday of each month with the exception of July and August and that shared interests would be explored, festive occasions enjoyed and sympathy and support offered when the occasion arose. In the early years the Limerick Branch had approximately 50 members but that number has now more than doubled. For the past decade meetings have been held in the South Court Hotel, with talks on various topics deemed appropriate for the retired members e.g. making a will, hearing loss and nutrition and fitness. The first Wednesday in November is always set aside as an occasion when deceased colleagues are remembered and their friends and relations are invited to participate. The December meeting is given over to the Christmas lunch, which again is held in the South Court Hotel.

Apart from the regular meetings at least two outings are arranged each year. Among the more interesting of these was a trip to Croke Park in April 2007, a coach tour of Galway's historic sites, a fun-filled lunch to Thomond Park, a visit to the Flying Boat Museum in Foynes followed by a visit to Listowel's Writers' Museum finishing with a spin on the heritage Railway.

In 2004 a group of members travelled to the Point Depot (later the O2 Arena) in Dublin for a performance of "Mamma Mia." The Limerick Branch has always been willing to get up and go. It has held numerous outings, which managed to combine educational and social activities. Not only have members visited the

Famine Museum on a rainy day but also enjoyed the more salubrious surroundings of Longueville House, Mallow, where they indulged in lunch but found out that the cost of refreshments was beyond the normal spend of retired teachers. The Limerick Branch hosted an extraordinary general meeting of the RSTA in February 2004. The purpose of the meeting was to revise the Rules of the association. This revision of the Rules had been prompted by the Limerick Branch, which had drawn attention to certain anomalies in the Rules then existing. The principal advocate for Rule change was Dáithí Geary. The EGM was held in the usual venue, the South Court Hotel, and was concluded successfully.

The Limerick Branch now has in excess of one hundred members. There is a very active officer board. When the founding secretary, Geraldine Reddan, became ill in 2002 Dáithí Geary was elected to replace her and when two years later, Tim Frawley stepped down from the chair he was replaced by Eileen Egan. Other members who have been active on the committee are Lelia Fitzgerald, Kathleen O'Sullivan, Hilda Rafferty and Sr. Marie Hayes. The current branch officers are Mary Finn, Chairperson, Denis O'Mahony, Vice-Chairperson, Mary Burke, Secretary, Mary O'Kelly, Treasurer, together with Dáithí Geary and Teresa McCarthy.[208]

Mayo Branch

The inaugural meeting of the Mayo Branch took place I the historic Daly's Hotel, Castlebar on 8th October 2001. Present were Margaret Naughton, Bríd Concannon, Pádraic Filan, Bernie Johnson and Kathleen Ryder. The hotel had originally been known as the Imperial and it was there in 1879 that Michael Davitt had founded the National Land League. The building is now in the ownership of Mayo County Council and has been converted for use as civic offices. Meetings of the Mayo Branch are now more usually held in the Mayo Education Centre with occasional forays to another historical location, Turlough House, which is now the home of the National Museum's Folklore Collections. The Mayo members are greatly appreciative of the facilities provided for them by the director and staff, with access to meeting rooms and computer rooms.

All of the founding members are still active in the branch and both Bríd Concannon and Kathleen Ryder have made outstanding contributions not only to the RSTA but also during their long teaching careers to the ASTI. Kathleen was forced to resign from her teaching post when she married following a directive in 1958 from the Catholic Archbishop of Tuam, which forbade the employment of married women in Catholic schools in the archdiocese. Even if she had succeeded in retaining her job there was no entitlement to maternity leave, nor were children's allowances paid to women. Kathleen took up the fight but it was not until Ireland became a member of the EEC in 1973 that the matter was finally resolved.

Branch activities have included talks from visiting speakers on a wide range of topics including retirement planning, wills and investments, healthy living, managing stress, University of the Third Age and the Citizens' Information Service. The branch also arranges classes on subjects of interest to members and these are always popular and well attended. Recent classes, which were presented by members of the branch, ranged from creative writing to digital photography, gardening and computers.

The activities of the branch have not been confined to talks and lectures. Visits have been undertaken to the Dáil and to Stormont and while visiting Belfast contact was made with retired members of NASUWT, which in turn led to a visit to the Titanic Centre in Belfast. The high point of the social calendar is the Christmas Lunch, which has been held in Ashford Castle and more recently in Lisloughrey where the branch was joined by members of other branches.

The Mayo Branch, which now has in excess of one hundred members, has been well represented on the national Committee. The Chairperson, Carmel Heneghan is currently Vice president of the RSTA and is also a member of the Equal Opportunities Committee of the ASTI. Muriel McNicholas is the National Treasurer of the RSTA while Denis O'Boyle is a member of the ASTI Pensions Sub-Committee. Another prominent member of the Mayo Branch is Bernie Johnson who was elected as Treasurer at the inaugural meeting and has been re-elected to that position ever since. The Vice Chairperson is Gabrielle Swift while Madeline Cunnane acts as Secretary with the assistance of Pat Walsh who acts as Public Relations Officer. From an RSTA perspective the West is very much awake.[209]

Midland Branch

The Midland Branch was established in November 2009 in Slashers GAA Club, Longford. Marie Doyle, RSTA President was the guest speaker. The original committee consisted of Pat Joe McLoughlin, Chairperson, Rosemary Kiernan, Treasurer, Martina Kelly, Secretary and Loreto Fahy, Assistant Secretary. This meeting would not have happened but for the fact that Sarah Scott of the National Committee had prepared the groundwork in advance. Sarah has served the RSTA loyally over the years as President, Treasurer and Organiser. Without her efforts there would have been no branch between Dublin and Sligo and it is due to her and Rosemary Kiernan that the inaugural meeting took place. While the first members were all from Longford it was always the intention that the branch would cater for retired secondary teachers not only in Longford but also in Leitrim, Roscommon and Westmeath and to welcome all who came. With that aim in view there has not been a permanent venue for meetings and while the premises of the Longford Slashers have been availed of meetings have also been held in the Education Centre, Carrick-on-Shannon and in Longford Library.

The branch, through its secretary, Martina Kelly, has made strong links not only with the National Committee of the RSTA but also with the local Citizens' Advice Bureau and particularly with the local media trough the Longford Leader, Cavan Celt, Leitrim Observer and Roscommon Herald.

While the branch is one of the youngest in the RSTA it can truly be said to have hit the ground running. In addition to the almost universal Christmas Lunch guided tours have been undertaken to Strokestown House, Carrick on Shannon and a two-night trip to Clare with a guided tour of the Burren with Hugh Carthy. The most adventurous outing was a visit to Moscow and St. Petersburg, which was undertaken n October 2012. Lectures on digital photography have been given by John Crowe and a workshop was held in Roscommon Arts Centre on the work of Gabhan Dunne. Pat Finnerty gave a presentation on his trip to Calcutta to undertake voluntary work and members have been instructed in the use of the library archives in Longford, not to mention a visit to the coal mines in Arigna. While branch membership stands at thirty it seems highly likely that it will grow considerably in future years.[210]

North Eastern Branch

The establishment of the North Eastern Branch RSTA can be traced to a meeting in the education centre, Chapel Street, Carrickmacross on 27th April 2004. This meeting was prompted by RSTA President Louis O'Flaherty, Pádraig Breathnach and Noel

Keane. O'Flaherty had been chairman of the Monaghan Branch ASTI some forty years earlier while Noel Keane had been a former Organiser and National Treasurer of the ASTI. Pádraig Breathnach had been a member of the Central Executive Council of the ASTI. Also at that meeting were Nuala O'Connor, Secretary RSTA and Catherine McHugh, Treasurer. Even though only seven local retirees attended the concept of establishing a local branch took root with a seed funding of €250 from central funds. The next meeting was held in the Imperial Hotel, Dundalk on Tuesday 22nd November 2005 with Art Agnew acting as chairperson but only six retirees attended. Because of the poor attendance it was decided to widen the net to include counties Monaghan, Louth and Cavan - hence the name the North Eastern Branch. Michael McMahon volunteered to contact school Principals and he also wrote directly to eighty-nine retired teachers in the three counties inviting them to a meeting in Carrickmacross on January 25th 2006. The meeting was held in the Fiddler's Boardroom. Twenty-four people were present and apologies were received from a further seventeen. The branch was effectively launched and Art Agnew, Michael McMahon and Caitríona McKenna volunteered to act as Chairperson, Secretary and Treasurer respectively for one year. On the suggestion of Tom Flynn it was proposed to invite former ASTI President Bernadine O'Sullivan to address the next meeting on matters relating to pensions, which she did on 8th March 2006. She was the first of a long list of speakers to address the branch at subsequent meetings. They have included Dermot Payne, Department of Social and Family Affairs, Richard Curran, Deputy Editor, Sunday Business Post, Tim Carey, author of history of Croke Park, Gerry Murphy, Met Éireann and Frank McNally of the Irish Times. Other speakers have included Michael Pitt, Fergus Nugent, John McArdle, John Scully, Kevin Gartlan and Moya Dillon.

Day trips incorporating lunch and a light evening meal have been organised by the branch and visits have been undertaken to Monasterboice, Drogheda, Dundalk, New Grange, Knowth, Carlingford and South Armagh. The Bronté Centre in Rathfriland and Downpatrick Cathedral have also been visited.

Other places visited include the Marble Arch Caves, Enniskillen Castle, Loughcrew and Inniskeen. Branch members have been joined on these outings by members from the Dublin branch and fraternal colleagues from NASUWT in Northern Ireland.

In addition to the lectures and local tours the branch has organised three short breaks over the years. The first and most notable was a trip to Barcelona in April 2007. In the same year a three-night break in Connemara with a day trip to Inis Mór was undertaken and the following year the branch arranged a mid-week break in Carrick-on-Shannon, which included a boat trip on the Shannon and a visit to King House in Boyle, Co. Roscommon.

Like other branches the Christmas lunch features largely in the calendar but not without a little sadness when it is remembered that founding members Tomás Mac Cathmhaoil, Aidan Harte, Hugh Hanlon, David Gallagher, Loretta Simpson, Pete Ward, Sr. Rita Greene and Tom Flynn have passed on. Despite the stated aim of Michael McMahon, Art Agnew and Caitríona McKenna in 2004 to stay in office for just one year just to see the branch safely launched, they are still office holders and continue to steer this vibrant branch.[211]

Sligo Branch

The first meeting of the reactivated Sligo Branch of the RSTA took place in the Southern Hotel, Sligo on 24th February 2009. Sixteen members attended the meeting including two Sisters from the Mercy Community, Sligo. The officers appointed on that day included Brendan Duggan, Chairperson, Máire Finan, Secretary, Tom Gilligan, Treasurer and Alice Lindsay, Assistant Treasurer. Following consideration of meeting dates already in place among teachers from various schools it was decided that the most suitable date for future meetings of the RSTA would be the first Wednesday of each month at 11.a.m. in the Southern Hotel, Sligo. This arrangement exists to the present day. The meeting was then addressed by Gerry Breslin, ASTI Standing Committee (more recently ASTI President) on the ongoing effects of the cutbacks on teaching posts in schools and on the pensions of retired members. Because of the uncertainty surrounding these cutbacks members invited Mr. Breslin to keep them advised on the efforts being made by the ASTI in terms of keeping the cutbacks to a minimum as they affected serving teachers as well as the pensions of retired members. This he did at the May and November meetings in 2009.

On 10th December 2009 ten members attended the Christmas Lunch in the Southern Hotel, which was a most enjoyable experience. In April 2010 a group of five members - Brendan and Carmel Duggan, Alice Lindsay, Vourneen Gallagher and Aileen O'Donnell went on a trip to Malta. Thanks to Ryanair and the ash cloud their pleasant holiday was extended by ten days at no cost to themselves. A trip to Stormont Castle, which would have included attendance at the Don McLean concert and an overnight stay in Belfast was organised for 10th May 2010 but had to be deferred at the last moment due to elections in Northern Ireland. Likewise a trip to Croke Park for members was also deferred for logistical reasons.

Christmas Dinner 2010 was held on 15th December, once again in the Southern Hotel, Sligo. Despite severely inclement weather fifteen members attended the dinner including the President, Marie Doyle who addressed the members on the effects of the imminent new Universal Social Charge, which would replace the Health and Income levies with immediate effect.

In August 2011 the Branch was proud to acknowledge the publication of a book of short stories entitled "Only a Rose and Other Stories" by its esteemed members, Mr. Lionel Gallagher. Lionel was a lifelong member of the ASTI. Having taught for three years in Sandymount High School, Dublin, he joined the staff of the Grammar School, Sligo in September 1959 where he taught until his retirement in 1997. Lionel holds the distinction of being the first student to obtain a University Scholarship from the Presentation Brothers' Secondary School, Carrick-on-Shannon, while his friend and classmate, the late John McGahern obtained the second such scholarship in the following year. Lionel has written on his connection with John McGahern in the Leitrim Guardian, 2010.

The RSTA meeting of 3rd November 2011 was attended by Mr. Shane Martin, psychologist, who addressed members on wellbeing for retired persons. Mr. Martin emphasised the need for a positive outlook on life in order to enjoy our years of retirement. The Glasshouse Hotel, Sligo, was the venue for the Christmas Lunch. It was held on 14th December 2011 with an attendance of twenty-four members and was a really enjoyable occasion.

During the early meetings of 2012 members expressed the view that they would benefit from a talk on the entitlements of retired teachers under the Social Welfare and other Acts. P.J. Leddy organised this talk to take place at the RSTA meeting on 5th September 2012. Ms. Orla Barry, citizens' Information Development Officer,

Sligo, addressed the members on the work of her Office which, she said, would be pleased to assist members in respect of any personal difficulties they might have with any Department of State. At this meeting also, Mary Mooney reported that she represented the Branch at the AGM of the RSTA in the Granville Hotel, Waterford on 1st May 2012.

Because 2012 was the 50th anniversary of the foundation of the RSTA it was decided that the Branch should mark the occasion by organising a number of trips to some of the following destinations: Áras an Uachtaráin, the Céide Fields, the Greenway Walking Route, New Grange, Kylemore Abbey and Gardens, the Model Arts Centre, Sligo (which presents musicals, poetry readings and exhibitions), Florence Court, Lough Key, Carrick-on-Shannon boat trips and the Hawk's Well Theatre Sligo.

The current Sligo Branch officers are Brendan Duggan, Chairperson, Máire Finan, Secretary and Alice Lindsay, Treasurer.[212]

Tipperary Branch

The minutes of the National Committee of the RSTA for 11th September 2001 record the intention to establish branches in a number of regional areas including Clonmel. Shortly afterwards members of the committee travelled to Thurles where they met with Pierce Purcell, former ASTI President 1973-74 and Noreen Woodlock who agreed to the establishing of a Tipperary Branch. They were given a small seeding grant but in the event the branch never really took off and the small sum was returned.

In late 2008 the National Committee set about trying to establish the branch. It was decided to host a lunch in Tipperary for all retired ASTI members who could be contacted in order to invite them to join the RSTA. The lunch was held in Hayes Hotel, Thurles on 29th April 2009 and was addressed by Louis O'Flaherty, Sarah Scott and Marie Doyle. The framework for a new branch was agreed.

The first meeting of the newly formed Tipperary Branch was held in Kearney's Castle Hotel, Cashel on 26th November 2009. At the meeting Mattie Finnerty, Cashel, was elected as Chairperson, Elizabeth Hayes, Cashel, as Secretary and Hilary Murphy, Clonmel as Treasurer.

The Highlight of the year is the Christmas lunch but other events and meetings are organised from time to time. One such event was a guided tour of the Rock of Cashel and a visit to Brú Ború.

The current membership of the branch is forty five. Mattie Finnerty is still the Chairperson and was elected to the National Committee at the RSTA AGM in 2012. Elizabeth Hayes is the Secretary and Richard Lowney acts as Treasurer. Other active members are Margaret Ryan-Niland, Catherine Crotty, Elaine Hannon and Phil Grace.[213]

Waterford Branch

In the spring of 2010 the then National Coordinator of the RSTA, Sarah Scott prompted John Cunningham to call a meeting of retired secondary teachers with a view to forming a branch of the RSTA in Waterford. Nine retired teachers attended. RSTA President Marie Doyle, Sarah Scott and Eileen Brennan of the National Committee came from Dublin. Marie Doyle immediately set about having an officer board elected that would form the nucleus of a committee.

Over the summer the officers prepared a programme of activities for the new branch. In September they hosted an inaugural reception in Waterford Teachers' Centre. The local ASTI Waterford Branch co-sponsored the event with the Teachers' Centre. Twenty-eight retired secondary teachers attended. They adopted the programme presented to them and elected three committee members to augment the officer board. Speaking at the reception the ASTI Branch Chairperson welcomed the forming of the RSTA branch. He said the ASTI branch had advocated such an initiative since Louis O'Flaherty first mooted it when he was President of that Association.

The members of the first committee of RSTA Waterford were John Cunningham, Chairperson, Kathleen Greene, Honorary Treasurer, Henry Collins, Secretary, Joan Martin, Martina Mannion and Siobhán O'Flaherty. At the 2012 AGM Kathleen Greene retired from her role as treasurer, to be replaced by Kieran McCarthy and Frieda Ryan joined the committee. Membership of the branch rose from the initial twenty-eight to sixty-nine and to eighty-two in subsequent years.

The Branch offers a varied programme of activities reflecting a broad range of interests of members. In the main, events are scheduled on a monthly basis. Staple features included annually are regular information and business meetings on pensions and related matters, outings to heritage sites, the annual festive lunch and the annual general meetings. Events have been held in Lismore and Dungarvan to honour an undertaking given at the inaugural meeting that activities would not be centred exclusively in Waterford City. Special interest events are arranged from time to time. Nine members went as a group on a mid-week theatre trip to London. Twenty-two members went on a four-day visit to Belfast. In Belfast the group visited Government buildings at Stormont and sat in on the Legislative Assembly. The centrepiece of the London trip was an extended tour of the Houses of parliament - members were in the Visitors' Gallery of the House of Commons for Prime Minister's Questions. Golf tournaments in Waterford and Dungarvan and weekly Wednesday morning boules sessions in the People's park also feature in the programme.

In May 2012 the Waterford Branch was honoured to host the Fiftieth Annual General Meeting of the Association. This was a major undertaking for the branch. The enthusiastic participation of members in the business meeting, the anniversary dinner and the associated cultural and social programme ensured it was a most rewarding experience for the hosting branch and its committee. The Mayor of Waterford invited the National Committee and members of the organising committee to a mayoral reception in City Hall to mark the occasion of holding the Fiftieth Anniversary AGM in the city. Louis O'Flaherty delivered the Anniversary Address at the Dinner on the evening of the Anniversary AGM. He spoke about the early years of the Association. Guest of Honour at the dinner was Joseph Lodge, son of the first President of the RSTA, George Lodge. George came from a prominent business family in Tramore, County Waterford.[214]

Wexford Branch

The first record of an intention to establish a branch in Wexford is in the minutes of the RSTA Annual General Meeting of 5th May 1999. At that meeting RSTA President, Seán Geraghty noted that the Galway Branch was thriving and that a branch had recently been established in Cork. He signalled the intention of members of the National Committee to travel to Limerick, Wexford, Waterford and Athlone for the purpose of assisting in the establishment of branches in these areas. While it is noted in the record that branches had been firmly established in Kilkenny and Limerick by March 2001 the question of how to organise a branch in Wexford was still being discussed in February 2001. Following a visit from members of the National Committee it is recorded in the minutes of the 2002 AGM that a branch had been established in Wexford. Dympna Gartland recalls being at her first meeting of the branch at the Talbot Hotel with just two other members, Seán Byrne, Chairperson and John Slevin, Treasurer.

Most of the activists of the branch are of a social nature and members are encouraged to bring friends or partners to events. During the summer time guided garden tours have been undertaken to places such s the Kennedy Park Arboretum, the Altamont Gardens in Tullow and Woodstock Gardens in Inistoige. These visits were usually followed by lunch in a local venue. In the wintertime the activities of the branch are more of an indoor nature with the Christmas lunch featuring highly. As Wexford has one of the most beautiful small opera houses in Western Europe it is not surprising that it has featured in the activities of the branch. One of the members of the branch, Megan O'Beirne, is a member of the Guinness Choir. Members have attended performances of Handel's Messiah and Bach's Christmas Oratorio in the Opera House while Megan has given an illustrated talk on Iceland. Other speakers have been Paul Turner who spoke on meditation, Nicky Furlong on the historic importance of Enniscorthy, Niall Wall on the connections between Newfoundland and the South East of Ireland and Billy Sweetman who gave two historical tours on 1798 and the significance of Vinegar Hill. Some of the members have walked the Camino de Santiago and Mary Kavanagh, Chairperson and Brigid McBride have given an illustrated account of their trip together with advice to intending walkers.

The regular meetings are now held in the Education Centre in Enniscorthy which provides a room and tea/coffee facilities. The centre also provides assistance with postage and the circularising of information to members. The centre has been of great assistance, particularly to the former secretaries, Dympna Gartland and Mary Kavanagh and the current Secretary John Dunbar. The branch is currently chaired by Margaret O'Neill and the Treasurer is Ailish Doyle.[215]

Wicklow Branch

In her bid to attract more teachers as they retired, Sarah Scott made it her mission as President of the RSTA to set up more local branches all around the country. On 5th November 2001, having put an ad in the Bray People and sent out invitations to people in the area, Sarah and five executives from the National Committee - Eileen Brennan, Sheila McGlynn, Seán Geraghty, Humphrey Twomey and Tony Burke - arrived in Bray to set up the Wicklow Branch. This inaugural meeting was attended by Eithne O'Brien, Breda Connolly, Esther De Groot, Esther G Hardy, Eileen Quinn, Rose Giblin, Vera Daly and Naula Carroll. Breda Connolly was elected Chairperson. Nuala Carroll agreed to act as secretary and Esther De Groot temporarily took on the role of Treasurer. Of the sixteen people who turned up that evening, including the two who responded to the ad in the Bray People, nine persons joined the new branch that night. The first meeting of the Wicklow branch was held in the Strand Hotel two weeks later on 19th November 2001.

It was clear from the beginning that the founding members were all keen to get involved in social activities; for example, in response to demand, Esther De Groot and Breda Connolly volunteered to lead guided walks around Wicklow, both being active walkers in the area. Information on topics such as travel and motor insurance was also keenly sought by members - this was investigated and the information shared by and between members. The social aspect of the group was deemed to be important. As it was a small group, members thought it might be a good idea to share ideas/activities with another branch. Contact was made with the Kilkenny branch, who very enthusiastically agreed to a shared meeting. Kay Sheehy, the dynamic secretary of Kilkenny arranged the joint meeting and lunch for 1st May 2002 at Hunter's Lodge in Mount Juliet, Thomastown. Wicklow branch members were given a right royal welcome by the Kilkenny members. It was more like a reunion of old friends than a meeting of new ones. The aims of the two branches were very similar, i.e. social ones. The return "joint meeting" was held in Woodenbridge the following autumn.

Finding volunteers to take on committee roles proved difficult from the start. Breda Connolly wore the two hats of Chairperson and Treasurer during the first two years. This was a particularly difficult task, especially as finances were very tight. At the AGM in 2003 it was decided that officers should be elected for a two-year period and that only two positions be filled in any one year. This alleviated the problem and for the next few years Jim Ryan took over the role of Treasurer and Aveen Kilduff was elected Secretary.

Meetings were initially held on the first Monday of every second month. The branch was particularly fortunate in that the Strand Hotel on Bray seafront very generously gave us the use of a room gratis for our meetings. While costs were therefore minimal the branch could not afford to host guest lecturers to talk to members. At that time, of the £18 annual membership fee paid by each member to the National Committee only £7 was returned to the local branch and this always seemed to be paid late in the year. Only in 2004 did the branch account come "out of the red!" Since then the financial situation improved as membership grew. Once the National Committee decided to increase the share of membership fees distributed to the local branches and paid that money in January it became easy to plan activities for the year.

Branch meetings are now held on the first Monday of the month in the Glenview Hotel in Glen of the Downs as this location is more central for members and there is ample parking space in the hotel grounds. The branch invites guest lecturers in to inform members on a variety of topics of interest. For example, a local solicitor gave an excellent talk on how to draw up a will, what pitfalls to avoid etc. The local Fire Brigade gave a very information talk on safety in the home. The branch has had outings to Kilcoole to study birds with "BirdWatch," and walks to the Devil's Glen and other beauty spots "among the Wicklow hills." There have also been visits to interesting and beautiful gardens like those of Lady Goulding, Mount Usher and the Botanic Gardens, guided tours of fascinating places like Charleville House and Garden near Enniskerry and Glasnevin Cemetery to learn some history. Doors have been opened on things to do, see and enjoy with good friends and companions

Branch meetings are suspended from June to September. To stay in touch during the summer months informal meetings are held on alternate Monday afternoons in the Mermaid Arts Centre in Bray for a cup of coffee/tea and a chat. These get-togethers have been very successful.

Each year the Christmas Dinner is held in Powerscourt Golf Club. This has proved a very successful celebration from the beginning as members, partners and guests are all greeted with a "welcoming drink" on arrival. The setting is beautiful and the dining room is ideal for this purpose - large enough to hold everyone comfortably yet small enough to make everyone feel "at home" in the hands of a very helpful and friendly staff.

The eleven years of the Wicklow Branch have been enjoyable and interesting ones. The branch has had its ups and downs but its enthusiastic and able officers have guided it well. Breda Connolly especially has been instrumental in keeping the momentum going over these years. Hopefully with a membership of 53 cordial individuals that momentum will continue into the future.

The current branch officers are Nuala Carroll, Chairperson, Eamon Madigan, Vice-Chairperson, Aveen Kilduff, Treasurer, Aileen Aherne, Honorary Secretary and Sheila O'Reilly, social Organiser.[216]

CHAPTER 12: CONCLUSION

When the RSTA was established in 1962 it was the first time that retired teachers took an active interest in demanding better conditions for retired members. Up until that time all demands for improvements in pensions were dealt with by serving teachers as part of the overall conditions of employment.

There had been a number of pension sub-committees in the ASTI over the years and some progress had been made by committed activists such as Cathal O'Gara but there had been no direct input by retirees until the establishment of the RSTA. That small gathering of retired secondary school teachers in the cramped offices of the ASTI in 36 St. Stephen's Green, Dublin on 26th March 1962 was to lead eventually to pension parity with serving teachers. It was a long road and none of the original founders of the RSTA were to live long enough to reap the full benefit of their endeavours. When pension parity was achieved more time became available for social activity. This was particularly evident from the 1980s when members from outside the Dublin area began to participate in greater numbers. The benefits of free travel were enjoyed and annual general meetings began to be held in places other than Dublin. The granting of Emeritus membership to retire ASTI members in 1982 was a seminal moment and strengthened the bonds between serving and retired teachers. The close relationship between the ASTI and the RSTA was reinforced during the presidency of Dónal Ó'Conalláin and was continued by subsequent presidents. The tension which arose in the mid 90s eased after a few years and was replaced with a more symbiotic relationship.

With the arrival of the new millennium serious questions were beginning to be asked about the ability of the State to fund future pensions. These matters were raised in a number of reports, starting with the Report of the Commission on Public Service Pensions 2000. These reports coupled with the experience learned from the implementation of he PCW in the 1990s led to the establishment of the ASTI Pensions Sub-Committee in 2004 in which RSTA members took an active part. Meanwhile the changed conditions of employment for secondary school teachers, which had commenced with the PCW continued into the new millennium. In 2002 teachers had voted to accept extra payment for supervision and substitution of students as part of a complicated deal to settle a salary dispute. Serving teaches could opt out of the scheme and forego the extra salary but many retired teachers who had carried out these duties without payment for many years and did not receive credit for their services in their pensions felt cheated.

With the collapse of the Irish economy in September 2008 conditions for all public servants and pensioners came under threat. Automatic entitlement of all those over 70 to a medical card was removed and replaced by a means-tested scheme. A universal social charge was introduced, as was a pension levy. Finally the starting salary for newly recruited teachers, of whom there were very few, was reduced by twenty percent. In these circumstances, the ASTI concentrated on trying to protect the conditions of the serving teachers. It may have been felt that the presence of a considerable number of retirees at the Annual Conventions of the ASTI was inappropriate, leading to the tabling of Motion 89 at the 2011 Convention. However, Motion 89, which sought to restrict the entitlements of Emeritus members of the ASTI was withdrawn and referred to a group overseeing all ASTI structures.

Through all of this, relations between the RSTA and the ASTI have been very good and are probably better than those which obtain in most other unions between their retired and working members. The ASTI arranges that all members of the RSTA receive copies of ASTIR and an annual pocket diary. It also provides a generous annual subvention and each December members are invited to a reception in Tomás McDonagh House. The two organisations have a parallel and supportive relationship, but like many relationships, not without tensions. There are differences. The RSTA admits retired members of religious orders while the ASTI Rules debar them from joining. The number of religious who have joined the RSTA is very small but they have contributed to the development of the association. The RSTA has no negotiating rights and must depend on the ASTI to defend its interests. This is still the position, as was ably demonstrated by George Lodge fifty years ago. In a time of crisis and recession it is natural that the energies of a union will be concentrated on protecting the interests of their paying members while being mindful of their retired members.

In the circumstances now prevailing it would be fair to say that the RSTA has reached the proverbial tipping point. It now has a membership larger than the ASTI had at its fiftieth anniversary. The very size of the organisation has meant that new administrative structures have had to be adopted. Demands on the honorary officers have increased and a system of making a small payment for expenses incurred has been introduced. The task of distribution of newsletters, which when membership was smaller could be undertaken by volunteers, has now been given to a commercial group. A new website has been established and an intensive recruitment campaign has been launched. As yet there is no permanent address and all communications must follow the location of the honorary officers. All of these matters have a financial implication and may require an increase in the annual subscription.

Not all members of the RSTA are Emeritus members of the ASTI, nor are all Emeritus members of the ASTI, who attend ASTI Annual Conventions, members of the RSTA. There is an overlap and the rights enjoyed by Emeritus membership of the ASTI are a concern for the RSTA. Proposals to restrict the role of Emeritus members have been on the ASTI agenda since 1996, as have proposals to restructure the RSTA as a branch of the ASTI. It is unlikely that these two issues will disappear and it is quite likely that they will be addressed in the Genesis Report, which is currently being undertaken, into the structures of the ASTI. The RSTA is now a considerably larger organisation than when these proposals first appeared and a different solution may be needed if both sides are to be satisfied. No matter how it is viewed it is to be hoped that the good relationship between the ASTI and the RSTA, which has existed over the last fifty years, will continue into the future.

APPENDICES

APPENDIX I

RSTA Presidents:

George Lodge	1962-1968
T.G. Boylan	1968-1971
Patrick Hardiman	1971-1982
Dónal Ó'Conalláin	1982-1988
Mona Hughes	1988-1990
George Lyons	1990 -1991 (died in office)
Maureen Gavin Duffy	1991-1992
Queenie Clohessy	1992-1994
Frank Campbell	1994-1996
Peter Kerr	1996-1998
Seán Geraghty	1998-2001
Sarah Scott	2001-2002
Humphrey Twomey	2002-2003
Louis O'Flaherty	2003-2008
Marie Doyle	2008-2011
Henry Collins	2011-

RSTA Honorary Secretaries:

Eva Quirke	1962-1969
P. Hanlon	1969-1981
A.J. Hannigan	1081-1982
Bríd Hanrahan	1982-1984
Anna Rigney	1984-1989
Frank Campbell	1989-1991
Maeve Colbert	1991-1995
Frances Clarke	1995-1997
Máirín O'Flynn	1997-1998
Eileen Brennan	1998-2000
Nuala O'Connor	2000-2004
Nuala Carroll	2004-2005
Marie Doyle	2005-2007
Eileen Kelly	2007-2010
Seán Fallon	2010-2012
Susie Hall	2012-

RSTA Honorary Treasurers:

A. Falvey	1962-1969
A.V. Henry	1969-1975
Eric Simmons	1975-1983
Tomás O'Riain	1983-1986
William Hanly	1986-1996
Éilís Delaney	1996-1998
Sarah Scott	1998-2001
Tony Burke	2001-2002
Catherine McHugh	2002-2008
Sarah Scott	2008-2010
Muriel McNicholas	2010-

The Pensioners' Case[217]

By George Lodge

President of the Retired Secondary Teachers' Association

First published in "The Secondary Teacher", February 1967

Despite the valuable verbal support given to us by our working comrades I feel that many young teachers, and even the not so young, would feel more sympathetic towards us if they saw our case against the historical background of the whole superannuation scheme. Although they give us their votes, I wonder would they be prepared to share with us any monies allocated to secondary teachers?

A salary scale for secondary teachers was not introduced until 1924/5 and there were not pension rights until 1929. Service prior to August 1925 is halved in calculating years of service and these years, along with service between 1925 and 1929 are reckoned at only one hundredth of retiring salary instead of one eighteenth. Because of these facts it is not fully realised that no teacher who retired before July 1965 could complete 40 years of pensionable service and retire on the full pension of half retiring salary. Even then he would have to have held a pensionable post since the age of 22 years and have given 43 years of service. A teacher who retired in 1957 having reached the age of 65 years and who was teaching in a pensionable post continuously from the age of 22 years would be allowed a pension of thirty-six eightieths of retiring salary. This was calculated as follows: From 1914 to 1925, 11 years, he would be credited with six hundredths. From 1925 to 1929 four hundredths, and from 1929 to 1957 twenty-eight eightieths making in all thirty-six eightieths of retiring salary. A single man or a woman with a pass degree would therefore qualify for a pension of thirty-six eightieths of £760 (or £342) and a married man with an Honours degree for thirty-six eightieths of £1008 (or £453 12s.). The budgets of 1962, 1963, 1964 and 1965 would have increased these figures to about £415 and £540 10s. respectively. Their slightly younger comrades who retired in July 1966, having reached the age of 65, and who began teaching at the age of 22 years in 1923 would have retired on their full maximum pensions of £635 and $855 respectively.

In August 1966 there were 430 retired secondary teachers drawing pensions; they were almost equally divided between lay and religious. The Department of

Education estimates the retiral rate at about 40 per annum, so that some 200 of these must have retired before February 1960, the salary scale to which all teachers' pensions were adjusted in the 1963 budget. Since all religious and a proportion of the lay teachers were retired on the unmarried scale, at least 120 of these retired teachers are trying to live on a miserable pension of about £400 per annum or £8 per week! No retired teacher qualifies for the contributory old-age pension, as British teachers do, and the means test debars them from the non-contributory pension. Quite a number of them also are helping to maintain invalid relatives. Mr. O'Malley, as Minister for Health, spoke very true words when addressing St. Ann's Guild in Limerick last June - he said: "As far as the old people of Ireland are concerned successive governments, including my own, have over the years been guilty of neglect."

Wage and salary increases to compensate for the spiralling cost of living are the order of the day for all sections of the community but one - pensioners. Since the 1965 budget adjusted our pensions to the consumer price index at February 1964, the cost of living has increased by over 15%. We did not share in Mr. Lemass's 12 per cent "prosperity bonus" of 1964 and we are considered in no budget proposals unless there is an unwanted surplus. Mr. Lynch gave us nothing in the 1966 budget, merely expressing regret that he had no money. Within three months, however, he was able to find money to increase salaries and wages of some 50,000 State workers, and a supplementary budget in the Autumn found money to compensate the milk producers. Whenever a demand is backed by sufficient force, money can be found; but the claim of Justice is insufficient in this so-called Christian land of ours. Let it not be thought that we pensioners begrudge wage increases where such are justified. We do not, but general increases in salaries worsens [sic] our position. Society must realise that, if it is not to create for itself a guilty conscience, it must make allowance for those whom it forces to cease working by compulsory retirement and for those who, through old age or illness, are unable to work.

The real cause of our trouble is that the money value of teachers to the community is being only slowly recognised and the work of those who retired before this recognition is valued in a debased currency. This is why we have the anomaly amongst nearly all State pensioners of men and women who gave the same service, often under worse conditions, existing on pensions much below the level of those paid to others who retired later. Teachers who retired since 1964 draw pensions 50% higher than their comrades who retired in 1960!

There are two reasons for this:- (a) Teachers were not paid the full value of their work in 1960 and (b) the value of the pound was less in 1964 than then, and it is worth still less today. This devaluing of money is likely to continue and you who may think your pensions satisfactory today will find them as little value relatively in seven years time as ours is now. What will ours be worth, if we are still alive, unless you help us do something about it now?

There is, of course, only one satisfactory remedy for this injustice: bring all pensions to parity with those currently retiring and thereafter adjust them pro rata with adjustments to salaries of serving personnel. This ideal is not new; indeed Great Britain and Ireland are amongst the very few countries where the principle does not obtain. In the "Report of the Committee on Post-retirement Adjustments in Public Service Pensions" - a document repudiated by the Joint Consultative Council of Retired State Servants - we read on pages 13 to 16 that parity is enjoyed in Austria, France, Belgium, Denmark, Luxembourg, Spain, Sweden and the United States. Dr. Ryan, speaking in the Dáil as Minister for Finance, in the debate on the Review of Pensions Motion on March 21st 1962 (Parliamentary debates Vol. 194, No. 2, cols. 247/8) said: "In present circumstances, therefore, people who retired 20 years ago find their pensions comparatively much lower than persons in a similar grade retiring now. Those in charge of the Exchequer might have been disposed at some time to say: 'We are fulfilling our contract and that is that; we shall not go any farther.' We, however, have departed from that . . . The only matter we need to discuss now is what we can do to bring them up to full equality with people retiring at the present time. I should like to be able to do it . . . the only thing that is preventing it is the cost." And again later in his speech: "I have only to repeat, so that there may be no misunderstanding, that, so far as the Government are concerned, we are sympathetic to the notion that pensioners should get an increase which will bring their pensions more into relation with the cost of living. I am doubtful that it could all be done in one bite . . ." Can this be construed as other than an acceptance by the Minister and the Government, which is still in power, of the principle of parity?

Successive ministers have pointed out that they have no money to see that justice is done to pensioners. Money has always been found, however, when the demand has been backed with sufficient force. The necessary money can come only from the country's earnings and these have been, however slowly, increasing. We do not accept this fatuous plea. There is money available, otherwise the growing expenditure could not continue. What is not available is the desire for justice; the decision to implement that section of the Constitution which says that: "The State pledges itself to safeguard with especial care the economic interests of the weaker sections of the community . . .." In common justice the Government must face the fact that pensions have an equal right to be included in the estimates with defence, education, agriculture, social welfare and all the rest. We are only asking for our rights. Our pensions are deferred pay and were meant to represent, when granted, a standard of living. A pension of £500 in 1966 gives only the same standard of living as a pension of £400 did in 1960 because of the devaluation of money. On top of this teachers and other State pensioners have been shown by arbitration courts to have been grossly underpaid in 1960, so that many pensions are reckoned on a salary that was unjustly low. These are the reasons why parity must in justice be applied. If our inclusion costs the State more, and the money really and truly cannot be found, then the solution is to give less all round, for surely there is no justice in letting the weaker members starve - that is jungle law not Christianity. Would you, our working comrades, treat us so? After all, there are some 4,300 teachers drawing incremental salary and we who number 400 on half pay represent only 200 more, less than 5%. For every £1000 the Minister finds he can allow to increase the pay of secondary teachers we ask but £45. I do not believe that you would begrudge us that. If the small deduction means so much to you, what does it mean to us to get nothing at all?

You must make the Authorities aware that you are really and truly behind our cause. You won Conciliation and Arbitration in 1951. Pension questions may be raised at conciliation level and although the subject is barred at arbitration level now, there is no reason why the methods that won arbitration for you cannot win its extension to pensions. Keep remembering that all of you will be pensioners some day, please God, and that our fight is yours. When you reach our stage you will be powerless, so act now while you can. We are not ungrateful for what you have done; we thank you sincerely for your help, and if we appear to be pressing you further now it is only because we know that the call of justice is not yet loud enough and that only force will tell. There is reason too to think that opposition is weakening before the growing support of workers.

APPENDIX II

Retired Secondary Teachers Association

Newsletter, November 1997

Confidential To Members

Dear Member,

We trust that this newsletter may clear up misunderstandings created by any unofficial communications, which you may have received.

Parity Campaign

What is "Parity"? Quite simply that increases paid to serving teachers in respect of salary, qualification allowances and remuneration in respect of duties attached to posts of responsibility be applied pro-rata to the pensions of retired teachers.

"A" Post holder B.A. (Pass) H. Dip. Ed. (Pass) with 40 years service is entitled to receive 50% of the increase awarded to "Assistant Principals" with the same qualifications and so on with regard to other posts.

The Committee is delighted that, with the exception of the £1,000 allowance, parity has been preserved, increases relating to posts of responsibility negotiated in the P.C.W. will be applied to your pensions.

Since the autumn of 1996, when it stood alone, the R.S.T.A., Officers, Committee Members and many drawn from the general Membership, has waged an unrelenting battle on many fronts to preserve the principle of public service pensions parity. The R.S.T.A. played a major part in supporting the campaign of the P.S.P. (Public Service Pensions) Action Group. Seán Geraghty and Michael Turner deserve a special vote of thanks for their efforts. We acknowledge too, with gratitude, the considerable impetus given to the campaign by the Private Member's Bill drawn up by the Labour

Party, which called upon the government to honour its pre-election promises by applying P.C.W. increases in re-structuring deals to public service pensions on the basis of full parity. This attracted cross party support from both houses with the exception of an independent senator from the T.C.D. constituency.

In the long run, the work of the Public Service Pensions Action Group, set up because of the inactivity of many major unions, was absolutely crucial to the final outcome. The P.S.P.A. mounted continual pressure upon the Rainbow Coalition and its Fianna Fáil/P.D. successors. It plotted strategy, kept the issue alive in the national newspapers. In May 1997 the P.S.P Action Groups Mansion House Meeting brought strong support from right across the whole spectrum of retired Public Service Workers. The P.S.P. Action Group organised demonstrations outside Dáil Éireann in October and November which caused the media to sit up and take notice and T.D.s to realise that the Public Service Pensions problem was not merely a burning issue, but a conflagration which threatened the credibility of the Government. It is highly unlikely that parity could have been preserved by any single public service pensioners association. We salute the Public Service Pensions Action Group, we salute all the public service pensioners who supported the R.S.T.A. To the R.S.T.A. Battalion we say "well done, but don't sheathe your swords, there may be other battles!"

Why Pensioners Should Not Be Deprived Of Parity

1. Parity of pensions was guaranteed by the Government in 1971 and 1986

2. Pensioners contributed to their Superannuation Schemes on that assurance

3. The Government now changes the goal-posts after the pensioners have paid their last contributions

4. Breaking parity will bring ANNUAL losses by 1 Sep. 1998 of £719 to £2,336 to, for example, secondary teachers who are now retired

5. On this occasion, it would take percentage increases up to 20% to compensate pensioners for the breaking of parity

6. The widows of public service pensioners on half-pensions will also be hit

7. The "productivity" and "restructuring" in the PCW Packages are bogus

8. In pleading for parity to be continued, pensioners are not asking for any increases per se in pensions but for their pensions not to be reduced

9. Pensioners had no voice in the negotiations that resulted in the threat to parity

10. The opposition politicians and union leaders who negotiated the breaking of parity are now calling for parity to be preserved

11. Bertie Ahern and Mary Harney promised before the last election that in Government they would restore parity

12. The breaking of parity contravenes the resolution of the European Parliament (24/2/1994) that Governments should not reduce pensions

13. At a time of economic prosperity and massive increases in tax-takes, there is no economic need to reduce public service pensions

14. It is inhumane to cut the pensions of the elderly and of widows

15. It is unjust to make the present generation of pensioners pay for any extra costs of pensions in the next century; future pensioners should pay for their own pensions.

16. It is unprecedented in Irish industrial relations to reduce pensions to pay for increases in salaries of those in employment (PCW Packages)

APPENDIX III

This is part of a very extensive file prepared by Michael Turner in 1997/98 to assist members of the RSTA and the Public Service Pensions Action Group (PSPAG) in their campaign to retain pension parity .

Why a retired teacher with 35 years service is entitled to benefit in his/her pension from the pensionable payment of £1,000 (plus) a year being paid to serving teachers with 35 years service.

1.   The payment of £1,000 (plus) a year requires of the serving teacher no extra work, no additional qualification, nothing except 35 years service, with 3 years of that on the maximum of the incremental salary scale (Document 6, PCW Package for Teachers). Therefore, a retired teacher with 35 years service and 3 years on the maximum of the incremental salary scale has the SAME ENTITLEMENT as that of the serving teacher to benefit in his/her pension from the payment in question.

   Educational innovation in Irish schools did not begin on 1 August 1996. The educational innovation undertaken over decades by teachers who retired before that date equalled or exceeded that expected of their successors from 1 Aug. 1996 to 31 July 1999.

2.   In all previous salary arrangements for teachers, every additional payment to a teacher on the maximum of the incremental salary scale was called a long-service increment, because IT IS AN EXTRA INCREMENT ON THE SALARY SCALE FOR LONG SERVICE. The £1,000 (plus) payment given to long-serving teachers in the PCW Package for Teachers is ENTIRELY based on a teacher being a specified length on the incremental salary scale. It would have been called, as previously, a long-service increment but it was labelled an "allowance" as part of a strategy to prevent pensioners from deriving any benefit from the PCW Package. An "allowance" for exactly what? Only for having 35 years service, with 3 years on the maximum of the incremental salary scale, which is precisely that of every retired teacher with that same service.

3.   Because of the Government decision on 4 Nov. 1997 to honour established parity, the Department of Education and Science and the Department of Finance are now allowing pensioners to benefit from other allowances negotiated in the PCW Package for Teachers. Why not from the "allowance" for long service?

4.   The Department of Education and Science, which has primary responsibility for teachers' pensions, HAS ALREADY ACCEPTED that a retired teacher can benefit in his/her pension from an allowance which he/she NEVER RECEIVED DURING SERVICE and on which the retired teacher COULD NOT HAVE PAID a pension contribution while serving.

At a meeting on 5 July 1971 between the Department of Education, the JMB and the ASTI to arrange for the then new posts of responsibility, "the Department officials stated that even if appointments or payment was not made by July 31st last the payments could be made retrospectively: those who retired on July 31st 1971 could, therefore, benefit for PENSION PURPOSES even if the payment was not made and even if appointments for 1970-71 WERE NOT MADE BY THE RETIREMENT DATE OF THE TEACHERS CONCERNED." (capitals added).

The Department cannot depart from this precedent of principle, not even if it has so far failed to find in its records individual instances of pensions having been paid on post of responsibility allowances to teachers who retired on 31 July 1971.

5.   As the Government decided on 4 Nov. 1997, public service pensioners should benefit in their pensions from the PCW increases in salaries to serving public employees. That decision is being contravened by the Department of Education and Science and by the Department of Finance operating a DISPARITY between the pensions of a teacher who retired BEFORE 1 AUG. 1996 and a teacher who retired AFTER THAT DATE, although both teachers had the same qualifications, the same posts and the same service.

6.   This disparity between pensioners being operated by the aforementioned Departments also contradicts the statement of the MINISTER FOR

FINANCE on the established parity between public service salaries and pensions. (Press release by Department of Finance, 4 Nov. 1997).

The Minister stated the Government position on parity as it has existed for secondary teachers since 1 Jan. 1973. Further, neither he, nor his Department, nor the Department of Education and Science has ever made a distinction for pensionability between scale salary and the allowances paid to teachers.

Parity, as stated by the Minister on 4 Nov 1997, is also the basis on which retired teachers paid their pension contributions. In addition, it is the basis on which they were told by the Department of Education and Science that their pensions would be paid (Information memorandum on secondary teachers' pensions issued by that Department).

7.   It is not a valid excuse for the Department of Finance to claim that, if retired teachers were allowed to benefit from the payment of the £1,000 (plus) being made to serving teachers, pensioners from the whole public service would also have to benefit. The arrangements for salaries and pensions in the various sectors of the public service are quite different. To substantiate its allegation, the Department of Finance has produced no figures for pensioners who retired before 1 Aug. 1996 from the various sectors of the public service in which pension entitlements are the SAME AS THOSE OF RETIRED TEACHERS.

In the case of the secondary teachers who retired before 1 Aug. 1996, they come from a small cohort of teachers who were recruited before Free Education was introduced in 1967 and not all of them had the required 35 years service. An actuarial study at the time showed that the survival of secondary teachers after retirement averaged one year. The average has since increased significantly, but the number of those who retired before 1 Aug. 1996 has also diminished substantially, and the number of those who are entitled to benefit from the payment of the £1,000 (plus) in question will eventually reduce to nil. In any event, as in other successful claims for compensation due from the Government, the claim of the retired teachers to benefit from the £1,000 payment should be determined on ENTITLEMENT, not on the numbers entitled.

8. The Department of Finance has also rejected the present claim of some pensioned teachers who retired before 1 Aug. 1996 because of the cost of allowing their claim. Again, the Department has disclosed no figures to sustain its rejection. The cost of allowing the claim of the retired teachers involved and of other public service pensioners with the same salary and pension arrangements cannot be burdensome at this time of unprecedented prosperity and of enormous and unexpected windfalls to the Exchequer revenues.

The cost of allowing this claim to probably a small number of pensioners becomes miniscule in the context of the real value of the public service pension contributions, which are in fact an annual, interest-free load by the contributors to the Government. Taking 1996 as a sample, the contributions of £178 millions at a modest 4% per annum over the 40 years of a normal career in the public service amount to £856 millions. What percentage of this would be the cost of paying FULL PARITY to the teachers retired after 35 years service?

If the pension contributions of secondary teachers had always been invested in trustee savings bonds, as stipulated in the 1929 Act setting up the Superannuation Scheme for Secondary Teachers, there would [be] a further significant contribution by teachers towards the cost of the claim by those with 35 years service who retired before 1 Aug. 1996. Like the number of claimants, that cost will in due course diminish to nil.

Again, the claim of the deprived pensioners should not be determined by cost, whether substantiated or not, but upon ENTITLEMENT.

Michael Turner.   29 Sep. 1998.

APPENDIX IV

The George Lodge 50th Anniversary Lecture

Louis O'Flaherty

Delivered at the AGM of the RSTA, Granville Hotel, Waterford, 2nd May 2012

Two events occurred in 1909, which were to have some significance on the future lives of secondary school teachers in Ireland. The first and most important was the founding of the Association of Secondary Teachers, Ireland, and the second was the introduction of the universal old age pension. Two of the principal aims of the ASTI were to secure an adequate salary scale and a pension scheme for teachers. Secondary school teachers in Ireland, at the beginning of the twentieth century, were in what we would now call a very bad place. They had no security of tenure and could be sacked at very short notice. They were often sacked for the duration of the summer holidays and re-hired in the Autumn. Unlike their colleagues in National and Vocational Schools they did not have any pension entitlements. This sorry state of affairs had come about because they were not employed by the state but by private employers who were mainly religious. Their conditions of employment were so bad that the Chief Secretary for Ireland, Augustine Birrell, speaking to the House of Commons on 23 May 1911 said: "The life of an ordinary assistant master in Ireland is detestable, the remuneration is miserably inadequate and he has no tenure of office." A similar view was expressed by Dr. Starkie, Chairman of the Intermediate Board of Education, when he said " Although many teach for a year, on the whole they are preparing for other work, no layman willfully takes up teaching as a permanent occupation."

While the universal old age pension did offer some hope to elderly people it was to be of dubious benefit to secondary school teachers. The pension was to be means tested at quite a low level and the hope of getting five shillings per week at seventy years of age did not give much encouragement to teachers to continue in their teaching careers in the precarious conditions that were then obtaining. It did of course lend greater strength to the case for a pension scheme for teachers. The nascent ASTI fought the cause of secondary teachers through the ensuing troubled times of lock-outs, rebellion, civil war, partition and economic ruin. In the process it managed to lose its Belfast Women's Branch, whose members were no doubt very happy when the benefits of the School Teachers (Superannuation) Act, 1918 were extended to them in 1922.

While the achievement of a satisfactory pension scheme was on the ASTI agenda since its inception in 1909, it was inevitable that in those times getting a decent salary scale, a Registration Council and security of tenure would always get priority in negotiations with the authorities. A salary scale was not achieved until 1924 and it was not until August 1929 that a pension scheme for secondary school teachers was introduced in the Irish Free State. Even the Minister for Education could not bring himself to enthuse about the scheme when he introduced it saying:

> I do not pretend that this scheme is over generous, and I am far from pretending that it will satisfy everybody. That is not the question. I think that any scheme that we adopt will be such as the resources of the country will permit.

The Minister, John Marcus O'Sullivan, never said a truer word. The scheme was to be voluntary and contributory with contributions from teachers, managers and the state. Benefits were to be calculated on the basis of one eightieth of retiring salary for each year of contribution and a notional one hundredth for each year of recognized teaching before the introduction of the scheme. There was no arrangement for parity with the salaries of teachers who were retiring at a later date so that when a pension was granted there was no system where by it could be increased to keep up with inflation or the decline in money values. The Irish Secondary School Teachers' Superannuation Scheme, despite some amendments did not become over generous in the following years. From its earliest days the ASTI had had a Pensions Sub Committee which strove to improve the pension scheme. Some improvements were achieved but the emphasis on pensions was always secondary to the demands for improved salaries. As already stated the pension scheme was both voluntary and contributory and as many teachers were very poorly paid they frequently deferred from joining the scheme.

In 1952 the Pensions Sub Committee of the ASTI proposed that a Pensioned Teachers' Association should be formed. This association would appear to have had a very limited life and while it did liaise with the ASTI on an ad hoc basis, by the late 1950s it was essentially moribund. In 1959 the Pensions Sub Committee commissioned an actuarial report into the benefits of the existing superannuation scheme. The final report was received in 1961. The report was a bit like the proverbial curate's egg. It was good in parts.

Without going into statistics it may be enlightening to consider the lot of one retired secondary school teacher in the 1950s. Alice Burnett had commenced her teaching career in the Holy Faith Convent in Chichester in 1908 but had returned to Ireland in 1915 and taught in a variety of schools until she secured a post in the Convent of the Sacred Heart, Leeson Street, Dublin in 1929, where she remained teaching until her retirement in 1951. On the 20 September, shortly after her retirement, she wrote to the ASTI stating that her pension, for the twenty years of her voluntary contributions, was £150 per year payable quarterly. At that time pensions were calculated on the average of the last three years of teaching and not just on the final year's salary. Even allowing for the fact that Miss Burnett had had a varied career pattern her pension was less than adequate and she instanced the fact that a medical officer would receive a pension of £500 per annum after 30 years service and a bank officer £200 after 20 years service. By 1958 her pension had increased to £172-3-0. Her correspondence makes for sad reading. When she first started her correspondence with the ASTI she was living in a small hotel in Harcourt Street and she was anxious to explain that that should not be taken as an indication that she was well off. Her last address was the Hospice for the Dying, Harold's Cross, Dublin to which the General Secretary of the ASTI wrote to her on 13 October 1959 informing her that her case had been raised with the Minister for Education but that nothing further could be done for her. It was in response to such cases that the Retired Secondary Teachers' Association was formed in 1962.

On the 23 March 1962 the newly appointed General Secretary of the ASTI, Ms. Máire MacDonagh, reported to the Standing Committee that she had circularized 50 retired teachers inviting them to a meeting on the 26th of the month for the purpose of forming a Pensioned Teachers' Association. This initiative had come in the first instance from the Pensions Sub Committee. At the next meeting of the Standing Committee on 6 April a letter was read from the newly established Retired Secondary Teachers' Association thanking her, Ms. MacDonagh, for the facilities provided and informing her that a committee had been formed with George Lodge as President and Eva Quirke, a former General Secretary of ASTI, as Honorary Secretary. The newly formed RSTA lost no time in getting down to business and held its second meeting on 16 April. The principal concern of the members was the inadequacy of their pensions. The RSTA did not have negotiating rights but they liaised with the Pensions Sub Committee through its chairman Cathal O'Gara. A common strategy was agreed between the ASTI, INTO and the Vocational Teachers' Association and was pursued through the aegis of the Irish Conference of Professional and Service Associations. The ASTI at that time had not yet become affiliated to the Irish Congress of Trade Unions. In November 1962 the three trade unions had agreed a joint agenda for negotiation on an improved pension scheme to be negotiated with the Department of Education. The principal objectives to be sought involved the granting of added years and an early voluntary retirement scheme in the case of disability. A demand for parity was also made so that the pensions of retired teachers should be equated to the salaries of those who were still teaching, thus if a teacher at the maximum of the scale should receive an increase of £200 the pensioned teacher with maximum service should receive an increase of £100. This was a very important issue as pensioners were paid pensions at a rate which was calculated on the salaries, which were paid at the time of their retirement and over time the cash value had been eroded due to the decline in the value of money and inflation.

At that time the RSTA was never much larger than a dozen dedicated members but they tirelessly lobbied their parent body. In a printed report in the ASTI Convention Handbook, 1964, George Lodge reminded delegates that the RSTA was affiliated to the ASTI and that all retired teachers should join the association. He went on to say that even though they were a small organization they exerted considerable influence through their association with the powerful Joint Consultative Council of Retired State Servants. He further stated:

> Not alone are you unwise not to join the Retired Secondary Teachers' Association but your self respect must suffer if you are prepared to stand aside and take what the work of your fellows get for you. Your association is affiliated to the ASTI thus giving the negotiators of that body authority to act also for you. Need I say more?

In 1964 the ASTI, in pursuit of a pay claim, refused to supervise or correct the state examinations. The members of the RSTA also refused to participate and one retired teacher went so far as to write to the Minister for Education stating that he was unwilling to act as an examiner. This was a brave stance as many pensioners were in quite straitened circumstances. George Lodge wrote to the ASTI saying that some form of compensation should be offered to those retired teachers who had refused to invigilate or correct papers. The ASTI did partially compensate some retired teachers, not all of who were members of the RSTA but in an accompanying letter urged them to join the RSTA as it was that organization which had espoused their cause.

All through the 1960s the disparity between pensions and the salary paid to serving teachers persisted. George Lodge continued to make the case for retired secondary teachers in every forum that was available to him. He participated in the preparation of a substantial submission prepared by the Joint Consultative Council of Retired State Servants to the Committee on Post Retirement Adjustments in Public Service pensions and challenged the report of that body in 1965. He sought a meeting with the Minister for Education to press the case for pensioners but was refused. He did everything possible to try and increase the membership of the RSTA but the numbers remained pitifully small.

In February 1967, The Secondary Teacher published an article entitled The Pensioners' Case by George Lodge. It was a comprehensive analysis of the plight of retired secondary teachers. In it he reminded those who were still working that the difficulties being experienced by retired teachers would be theirs at some time in the future and when that day arrived that they would be powerless unless they had the support of serving teachers.

Some weeks later, speaking at the Annual General Meeting of the RSTA on 22nd March, 1967 he said that it was difficult to see how a Minister for Finance could go on handing out the same old plea, that there was no money available, when time after time he was able to find money when the claim was backed up with sufficient force. He went on to say:

> If our Christianity and our civilization mean anything, every
> man should feel that justice will be done to him by society just

as he expects justice within the narrower limits of his own family. If Christians are brothers in Christ the weak should be able to expect just treatment as surely as the weak ones expect it in the family circle. Jungle law must give way to the reign of justice coupled with mercy if Christianity is to survive.

He went on to bemoan the fact that so many retired teachers were still outside the ranks of the RSTA and attributed this to an attitude of "I'm alright Jack". He said that due to the absence of parity, some of those who had more recently retired had pensions far in excess of those who had retired at an earlier time. He repeated what had become his mantra - that it was the same small group that had kept the association going and he wondered aloud if they were the only ones who wanted to keep the RSTA alive. He concluded his speech by saying that if the RSTA was more strongly supported they could make the AGM a more social occasion. He mused that it would be nice if they could afford to have a little standing buffet for the one night of the year and be able to meet one another on a more social footing. The tone of his speech was remarkable reflecting elements of deep religious conviction, social solidarity, commitment, frustration and regret.

At that time George Lodge was seventy-four years old. He had been born in Tramore, County Waterford in 1893. He won a scholarship to the Royal College of Science, Ireland in 1912 and graduated in 1916. After graduation he went to work as a research chemist at Levinsteins, dyestuffs manufacturers in Manchester. While there he played a significant part in the escape of Austin Stack and Piaras Béaslaí from Strangeways Jail in October 1919. He had provided the taxi to transport them from the prison and had sheltered them in his home. In 1920 he returned to Dublin and the following year he got a job teaching physics and chemistry in St. Columba's College, Rathfarnham, which would have had a very different ethic and philosophy from St. Enda's which was located not too far distant. It would seem to have been a most unusual choice of school for a young man with his kind of experience but no doubt a position was available and he was well qualified to get it and it is most unlikely that the management of St. Columba's was aware of his adventures in Manchester. By a curious coincidence one of the small group who founded the RSTA was Brian Joyce, a native of the Aran Islands who had been educated at St. Enda's and who as a student in 1916 had been in the General Post Office with Patrick Pearse. Whatever story lies behind George Lodge getting the job in St. Columba's he was to remain there until he retired in 1959. From 1960 he lectured on teaching methods to students for the Higher Diploma in Education in University College Dublin, no doubt to supplement his rather meagre pension. During his long teaching career he had published school texts on Physics and Chemistry and had also been one of the founders of the Irish Science Teachers' Association and in which organization his memory is still honoured.

Despite his plea for new members at the 1967 AGM the numbers in the RSTA remained small. The sense of increasing frustration is apparent in his report to the 1968 ASTI Convention. He noted that the RSTA had been unrepresented at a recent important meeting of the Joint Consultative Council of Retired State Servants because he was in hospital and another member of the committee was ill and they were unable to find substitute delegates. He regretted that some retired secondary teachers were holding jobs in vocational schools but they could not attend meetings of their own organization. They were quite prepared to sit back and draw whatever benefits accrued from the hard and unselfish work of the small RSTA group. This was the last report submitted by George Lodge. His health had been failing and he died in September 1968.

In the RSTA report to the 1969 ASTI Annual Convention, the new president of the RSTA Mr. T J Boylan noted his passing and that of Eva Quirke, the two initiators and founders of the RSTA and said:

> Each of them worked unceasingly for the advancement of our cause and their passing was a grievous blow to their colleagues. Even when George was sinking fast he constantly thought of the RSTA. In the last conversation I had with him he expressed the hope that the association should flourish and that our work should be crowned with success. Let us all join together to ensure that the last wish of our founder and president be fulfilled.

I believe that our presence here this evening is evidence that his wish has finally been fulfilled.

Ní bheidh a leithéid arís ann!

ENDNOTES

1 John Coolahan: "The ASTI and Post Primary Education in Ireland 1909-1984"

2 I.S.W., 27th February 1926, LXXIX, P.258

3 I.S.W., 27th February 1926, LXVII, P.258

4 John Coolahan: "The ASTI and Post Primary Education in Ireland 1909-1984"

5 "Dáil Debates" Vol 25, 18th July 1928, p.p. 6-10.

6 John Coolahan: "The ASTI and Post Primary Education in Ireland 1909-1984" p.102

7 John Coolahan: "The ASTI and Post Primary Education in Ireland 1909-1984" p.164

8 Ibid. p.165

9 ASTI Archive LHS File No. 179

10 ASTI Convention Handbook, 1964, p.97.

11 Standing Committee 15/06/1964.

12 ASTI Annual Convention Handbook, 1965, p.

13 See Appendix 1.

14 RSTA President's Address, L.H.S., ASTI Archive, 176.

15 Ibid.

16 ASTI Annual Convention Handbook Section VIII, 1967.

17 Standing Committee minutes May 4th 1968.

18 Standing Committee, March 22nd 1969.

19 ASTI Convention Handbook, 1970, P.85.

20 Standing Committee minutes December 4th 1971 and January 22nd 1972.

21 ASTI Convention Handbook 1973, Section VI, p. 61.

22 Standing Committee minutes January 19th 1974.

23 Minutes of RSTA Committee Meeting, March 28th 1974.

24   Ibid.

25   ASTI Convention Handbook, 1974, Section VIII, P. 96.

26   ASTI Convention Handbook, 1975, Section VIII P.131.

27   Ibid.

28   RSTA Minutes March 7th 1975.

29   RSTA Minutes, December 8th 1975.

30   RSTA Minutes, July 14th 1978.

31   Ibid.

32   Report of Meeting of Retired Secondary Teachers held at 13, Highfield Rd., Rathgar, Dublin, September 29th 1981 - ASTI Archive L.H.S. File 179.

33   Minutes of Meeting of September 29th 1981. RSTA Archive.

34   Minutes of Meeting November 10th 1981. RSTA Archive.

35   ASTIR, February 1982.

36   ASTI Convention Handbook 1982, p.140.

37   Report of Annual Convention 1982.

38   Ibid.

39   ASTIR, February 1984.

40   Ibid.

41   ASTI Convention Handbook, 1983, pp. 66-67.

42   Minutes AGM RSTA, March 28th 1984.

43   RSTA Minutes, June 6th 1984.

44   RSTA Minutes, AGM, March 22nd 1985.

45   RSTA Minutes, November 27th 1985.

46   RSTA Notes, ASTIR, May 1985.

47   Minutes, RSTA AGM, April 29th 1987.

48   Minutes, RSTA AGM, April 25th 1990.

49   RSTA Minutes, November 21st 1991.

50   Cunningham, John: "Unlikely Radicals" . . .

51   Minutes, RSTA, November 21st 1991.

52   Standing Committee, September 30th 1991.

53   Minutes, RSTA, January 15th 1992.

54   RSTA, AGM, Minutes, April 29th 1992.

55   RSTA Minutes, January 20th 1993.

56   RSTA Minutes, October 19th 1994.

57   Minutes, Annual Convention 1982.

58   Report of the Biennial Conference ICTU 1995

59   ASTI Annual Convention Handbook, 1997, pp. 312-313.

60   ASTI Annual Convention Handbook, 1996, pp. 13-18.

61   Ibid. Motion 164.5, p. 15.

62   RSTA Minutes, January 18th 1995.

63   ASTI Annual Convention Handbook, 1995, Section IX 22.4, P.312.

64   Report of Meeting with RSTA Representatives, September 19th 1995, Standing Committee Minute 233/95.

65   Letter from Pat King to Frances Clarke, Oct 18th 1985.

66   Letter from Frances Clarke to Pat King, undated, marked "received Oct 23rd 1995," RSTA Archive.

67   Letter from Pat King to Frances Clarke, Oct 24th 1995.

68   Standing Committee minutes, Sub-Committee C Nov 17th 1995.

69   ASTI Annual Convention handbook 1996, pp. 13-19.

70   Ibid. pp.164-165.

71   RSTA minutes, March 30th 1996.

72   Minutes, RSTA AGM, Galway, April 17th 1997.

73   Minutes RSTA Committee Meeting, June 3rd 1997.

74   Minutes of RSTA Committee Meeting May 19th 1996

75   Appeal to CEC by the RSTA January 11th 1997, RSTA Archive.

76   ASTI Nuacht Special Edition, January 1997.

77   Ibid. P.4, 3.2.

78   Ibid.

79   Michael Turner file in RSTA archives.

80   Minutes, RSTA AGM, April 17th 1997.

81   Minutes, RSTA committee meeting, June 3rd 1997.

82   Ibid.

83   RSTA Archives.

84   Ibid.

85   Letter from Máirín O'Flynn, June 7th 1997, RSTA FILE Documents 1997-1999.

86   RSTA Archive File, Documents 1997-1999.

87   Letter, Michael Turner to Seán Geraghty, August 25th 1997, RSTA Archive File Documents 1997-1999.

88   Letter, Charlie Lennon to Seán Geraghty, September 30th 1997, RSTA Archive File 1997-1999.

89   Minutes of RSTA EGM October 23rd 1997.

90   Letter, Michael Turner to Seán Geraghty, October 27th 1997, RSTA Archive File 1997-1999.

91   Ibid.

92   Letter, Charlie Lennon to Seán Geraghty, February 12th 1998, RSTA Archive File 1997-1999.

93   Unpublished tribute to Michael Turner by John O'Sullivan.

94   "The End of Pension Parity?" RSTA Archive, Michael Turner File.

95   Minutes, RSTA AGM, May 5th 1999.

96   Minutes, Committee Meeting 19th May 1996.

97   Minutes, RSTA Committee Meeting, 3rd June 1997.

98   Minutes, RSTA Committee Meeting, 30th June 1997.

99   Ibid.

100   Minutes of RSTA EGM, 23rd October 1997.

101   Ibid.

102   Letter, Charlie Lennon to Seán Geraghty, 30th September 1997.

103   Letter, Charlie Lennon to All RSTA Members, 14th October 1997.

104   Minutes, RSTA EGM, 23rd October 1997.

105   Ibid.

106   Letter, Michael Turner to Dan Kelly, 27th October 1997 - RSTA Documents 1997-1999.

107   Ibid.

108   Ibid.

109   How a Simple Deal for Teachers Went Off the Rails: Louis O'Flaherty, Irish Independent, 1st April 1996.

110   Letter, Margaret Stewart to Seán Geraghty, 8th September 1997 - RSTA Documents 1997-1999.

111   Minutes, RSTA Committee Meeting, 12th November 1997.

112   Minutes, RSTA Committee Meeting, 14th January 1998.

113   Minutes, RSTA Committee Meeting, 29th September 1998.

114   Minutes, RSTA Committee Meeting, 7th January 1999.

115   Ibid.

116   Minutes, RSTA AGM, 5th May 1999.

117   Ibid.

118   Minutes, RSTA Committee Meeting, 7th September 1999.

119   Minutes, RSTA Committee Meeting, 3rd November 1999.

120   Ibid.

121   Minutes, RSTA Committee Meeting, 9th February 2000.

122   Minutes, RSTA AGM, 8th May 2002.

123   Ibid.

124   Minutes and Report of ASTI Special Convention on Pensions, 2nd October 2004.

125   Ibid., p.7.

126   Ibid., p.8.

127   Letter, Louis O'Flaherty to Hon. Branch Secretaries, ASTI, 19th January 2005.

128   Minutes, ASTI Pensions Sub-Committee, 27th September 2006.

129   Minutes, ASTI Pensions Sub-Committee, 19th May 2008.

130   ASTI Response to the Green Paper on Pensions (undated).

131 Minutes, ASTI Pensions Sub-Committee meeting, 10th March 2009.

132 Minutes ASTI Pensions Sub-Committee, 30th April 2009, as amended 16th June 2009.

133 Minutes, meeting of ASTI Sub-Committee on Pensions, 18th November 2009.

134 Report of Pensions Sub-Committee, ASTI Convention Handbook, 2010.

135 Report for the Association of Secondary Teachers, Ireland/Irish National Teachers' Organisation/Teachers Union of Ireland - Future Pension Provision 2010, p.5.

136 ASTI Convention Handbook, 2012, Book II, p.22.

137 Minutes, meeting of Pensions Sub-Committee, ASTI, 4th December 2012.

138 Minutes, RSTA AGM, 7th May 2003.

139 Ibid.

140 For detailed account see "Unlikely Radicals," John Cunningham, Cork University Press, Cork, 2009.

141 Minutes, ASTI CEC Meeting, 22nd January 2000.

142 "Unlikely Radicals," John Cunningham, Cork University Press, Cork, 2009, p.278.

143 Ibid., p.295.

144 Minutes, RSTA Committee Meeting, 11th June 2001.

145 Minutes, RSTA Committee Meeting, 19th February 2002.

146 Letter, Pádraig Maloney, Principal Officer, DES to Nuala O'Connor, Hon. Secretary RSTA, 8th October 2003.

147 Ibid.

148 Minutes, RSTA AGM, 7th May 2003.

149 Ibid. The members mentioned were Bernadine O'Sullivan, Susie Hall, Máire Ní Laoire and Helen Breathnach.

150 "The Stealth Attack on Public Service Pay and Pensions," Bernadine O'Sullivan, RSTA Files.

151 Ibid.

152 Minutes, RSTA AGM, 3rd May 2004.

153 Minutes, ASTI Special Convention, 2nd October 2004, p.7.

154 Ibid.

155 Ibid.

156 Ibid.

157 Minutes, RSTA Committee Meeting, 6th October 2004.

158 Minutes, RSTA AGM 2004.

159 Report, ASTI Annual Convention, 2003.

160 Report, ASTI Annual Convention, 2004.

161 Minutes RSTA Committee Meeting 19th January 2005.

162 Minutes, RSTA Committee Meeting, 19th April 2000.

163 Minutes, RSTA AGM, 2nd may 2007.

164 Minutes, RSTA Committee Meeting, 9th April 2008.

165 Minutes, RSTA AGM, 17th May 2008.

166 Ibid.

167 Minutes, RSTA AGM, 6th May 2009.

168 Memo of Meeting, 1st July 2009, RSTA Files.

169 Minutes, RSTA Committee Meeting, 28th January 2010.

170 Ibid.

171 Minutes, RSTA Committee Meeting, 24th February 2010.

172 Minutes, RSTA Committee Meeting, 26th April 2010.

173 Minutes, RSTA AGM, 5th May 2010.

174 ASTIR, September 2010.

175 Minutes, RSTA Committee Meeting, 22nd September 2010.

176 Ibid.

177 RSTA Newsletter, Christmas 2010.

178 Minutes, RSTA AGM, 4th May 2011.

179 Minutes, RSTA Committee Meeting, 7th November 2011.

180 Ibid.

181 Minutes, RSTA Committee Meeting, 24th January 2012.

182 RSTA Newsletter, Autumn 2012.

183 Ibid.

184 Ibid.

185 RSTA Newsletter, Winter 2012.

186 Minutes, RSTA Committee meeting, 10th November 1981.

187 RSTA Notes, ASTIR, February 1982.

188 RSTA Notes, ASTIR, November 1982.-

189 Minutes, RSTA Committee meeting, February 1984.

190 RSTA Notes, ASTIR, October 1984.

191 RSTA Notes, ASTIR, December 1984.

192 RSTA Notes, ASTIR, April 1985.

193 Minutes, RSTA National Committee Meeting, 24th June 1992.

194 Minutes, RSTA National Committee Meeting, 18th November 1992.

195 Minutes, RSTA AGM, 28th April 1993.

196 Minutes, RSTA National Committee meeting, 22nd June 1995.

197 Minutes, RSTA AGM, 3rd May 2000.

198 Minutes, RSTA National Committee meeting, 11th September 2001.

199 RSTA Notes, ASTIR, February 2002.

200 Ibid.

201 RSTA Notes, ASTIR, April/May 2002.

202 RSTA Notes, ASTIR, May 2003.

203 Based on RSTA records and memos supplied by Pat Browne and Humphrey Twomey.

204 Based on RSTA records and memos supplied by Gerard Logue.

205 RSTA records and memo from Bláithín Ní Bhric.

206 Details supplied by Claire Power.

207 RSTA records and Memo from Kay Sheehy.

208 RSTA records and memo from Mary Burke.

209 RSTA records and memo from Carmel Heneghan.

210 RSTA records and memo from Martina Kelly.

211 RSTA records and memo from Michael McMahon.

PSPAG:	Public Service Pensions Action Group
RPSEA:	Retired Public Service Employees' Association
RSPA:	Retired State Pensioners' Association
RSTA:	Retired Secondary Teachers' Association
RSTB:	Retired Secondary Teachers' Branch
RSTI:	Retired Secondary Teachers', Ireland. An earlier name for RSTA
SC:	Standing Committee of ASTI
TUI:	Teachers' Union of Ireland
UCD:	University College Dublin
VTA:	Vocational Teachers' Association

INDEX

INDEX

W